Crime Prevention
for Houses of Worship

by

Chester L. Quarles, CPP, and Paula L. Ratliff

American Society for Industrial Security
1625 Prince Street
Alexandria, Virginia 22314

NOTE: The symbols on the cover of this book represent six of the major world religions: Christianity, Buddhism, Judaism, Islam, Hinduism, and Confucianism.

Copyright 2001 by the American Society for Industrial Security

ISBN 1-887056-13-0

Printed in the United States of America

10 9 8 7 6 5 4 3 2 1

ACKNOWLEDGMENTS

The completion of this work is an answered prayer for us. We have researched this topic for several years, and have seen more and more violence and destruction take place in our religious institutions. We have watched congregations as they have tried to contravene these destructive and violent events and as they worked through hurt, anger, shock, and fear. Our goal in this effort is to raise the awareness level of each religious administrator, pastor, priest, and rabbi, and to reduce the potential for victimization.

We are grateful to our family, friends, and colleagues who have encouraged, guided, and sustained us. We are grateful for their love and support.

Chester L. Quarles and Paula L. Ratliff

FOREWORD

On September 15, 1999, a crazed gunman entered into Wedgwood Baptist Church in Fort Worth, Texas. What started as a Youth Rally Praise and Worship Service ended in a blood bath that took the lives of seven young people and left seven others wounded. The gunman's hand was forced and he ended the spree by taking his life, but not before changing the lives of hundreds forever. That was and still is my church, where I serve as a deacon and adult Sunday school teacher. I am also a Fort Worth police officer and happen to live across the street from the church. My wife is our pastor's secretary and had just walked out of the worship center when the gunman walked in shooting. My fifteen-year-old daughter was in the worship center, along with about four-hundred-and-fifty other youths and sponsors.

How could all of this have been prevented? What could have been done to stop the killings? Are churches just as vulnerable as the rest of society to the wanton acts of violence? Aren't we safe at church anymore? No, we are not!

Fourteen years as a police officer have afforded me many unfortunate opportunities to visit crime scenes. In many of those situations, the crime could have been lessened in impact or altogether avoided if some kind of deterrent had been implemented. Worship facilities are no longer sacred places and are becoming more and more the target of choice for the criminal who is looking for an easy target. Crime statistics show a steady increase in property crimes and crimes against persons taking place on church owned property. In some situations, the lack of basic and prudent security measures can be grounds for civil liability.

Dr. Quarles and Ms. Ratliff assemble in this book the most effective and current information available to church leaders who want to be effective in their ministries by being diligent in their efforts to protect their congregations. This book is a comprehensive manual and guide to the effective use of the resources that are available to you in your efforts to deter crime at your church. Whether you are in the planning stages for your facilities or you are just interested in making your buildings as safe as possible, this book is what you will need to get the job done.

There are things that you can do to help safeguard your church or worship facility. This book is one of the best tools I have seen to help you make a plan for the overall safety of those you worship with and the place you worship. For you to choose to do nothing about security may be the more criminal act.

Corporal S. M. "Chip" Gillette
Fort Worth Police Department
Fort Worth, Texas

DEDICATION

Dedicated in loving memory to my mother,

Helen Burns Ratliff,

whose love continues to hold and sustain me.

Paula

Dedicated to my loving wife,

Dorothy Ann Denham Quarles.

Chester

TABLE OF CONTENTS

Part I: *Introduction to Security*

Chapter 1

Chapter 2

Part II: *Protecting Property*

Chapter 3

Chapter 4

Chapter 5

Chapter 6

Chapter 7

Chapter 8

Part III: *Protecting People*

Chapter 9

Part IV: *General Crime Prevention*

Part I:
Introduction to Security

CHURCH CRIME OVERVIEW

The chilling reality of our times is that violent, often deadly, acts are being perpetrated against innocent people, including children, as well as community institutions. The dangers posed to synagogues and churches, schools, commercial and public buildings, and to entire communities of people are a matter of record.[1]

Increasingly, worship centers are being targeted by criminal predators. Congregations are more at risk than ever before in the United States. The criminals prey in the parking lots and in the worship facilities. Whether a congregation follows the Bible, the Koran, or the Talmud, there are many similarities of worship patterns, even though the religious viewpoints differ considerably. Crime prevention approaches are very similar whether we are dealing with crime at a church, a mosque, a synagogue, or a temple.* The greatest weakness in the religious setting is the mind-set of those attending. We visit houses of worship to pray, sing, contemplate, and worship—not to think about crime. Worshipers are intent on prayer and worship and are less focused, perhaps, to the crime risks contemporary to our time.

Perhaps the greatest crime committed against houses of worship is the loss of faith, as well as questioning honesty, integrity, and the American lifestyle. Saul Astor, a leading crime prevention expert, had this to say about how thieves and other predators influence us in his book, *Loss Prevention: Control and Concepts*:

> Let's keep criminals out of our (institutions) and out of our lives. Criminals destroy our faith in each other. They threaten our livelihoods. Let's not be deceived by them. Let's learn to recognize them and to drive them from our midst![2]

Believers find it difficult to even imagine the deviant mind-set necessary to commit a crime at a house of worship. We enter our house of worship with a feeling of awe and reverence, believing these to be sacred and hallowed grounds. As we begin our prayers, songs, and readings, we listen and are submissive to a higher power. We are there for healing, guidance, and hope.

*The term "church" will be used most often in this material. However, the co-authors intend the term to include all "houses of worship," no matter what the focus or creed. In this regard, the crime prevention, crime avoidance, and crime deterrence approaches can be applied to the unique culture of every religion or denomination.

However, to the deviant mind, there is nothing sacred—not one single thing, or place, or creed, or set of beliefs. Criminals usually have no fear of "judgment" as they search for an easy victim. Our places of worship offer large rewards for the criminal looking for an easy victim, unless numerous crime prevention approaches are in place. Our facilities offer worshipers who are unsuspecting and unarmed. They bring cash offerings and are dressed in their best, often with jewelry and furs. Our parking lots are filled with cars and trucks with expensive radios and car phones. There is property to be taken, infants or children to be abducted, girls or women to be abused or raped, and many fairly passive victims—the old and infirm, the young and dependent, the unarmed and the unsuspecting.

Many congregations do not have police officers as members. Our research has indicated that police officers who frequently attend church often leave their guns at home because they do not want to offend people at church who might think less of them for carrying weapons into the place of worship. Realizing that some people fear weapons, the officers choose to leave the weapons behind.[3]

Crimes That Have Occurred in Houses of Worship

- A nun was strangled in the church garden.
- Worshipers were robbed at gun point during the services.
- An emotionally disturbed man took a congregation hostage and held them in a confrontation with police.
- A deranged man drove his truck though the church doors during services.
- A woman praying was assaulted, robbed, and raped in the sanctuary.
- A pastor was assaulted with a baseball bat.
- A pastor was shot in his front yard simply for counseling the abused wife of a violent husband.
- The church offering disappeared after the treasurer was distracted from the counting room.
- A deranged gunman killed several teenagers during a special service.

The increase in violence in places of worship and the vulnerability of our religious facilities prompted us to write *Crime Prevention for Houses of Worship*. This book will demonstrate common-sense approaches to crime deterrence. It is the authors' intention to help you plan crime avoidance programs at your church, mosque, synagogue, or temple. We encourage proactive approaches to help avoid or deter situations in which you must react to the trauma of crime. We will provide guidance on both.

There are several steps necessary to reduce the risk of crime at your facility. The first step *is to stop denying that crime occurs in houses of worship.* You need to accept the fact that crimes occur at religious facilities, regardless of size, location, religion, or denomination. The second step is *take charge of your facility. You must accept the fact that the police may be unable to prevent an attack and may not be there when a crime occurs.* Depending on the type of crime, they may not be able to solve it, unless YOU are able to provide substantial evidence to assist in the investigation, arrest, and subsequent prosecution. The third step is *to recognize that you can do something about crime by taking action and implementing the suggestions offered in this book.* This book can't help you secure your facility unless you decide to take action.

Houses of worship are rarely the focus of security or crime prevention efforts. Clergy typically are not aware of vulnerabilities and basic crime prevention methods. Simply put, many houses of worship are easy prey.[4]

This book will help the clergy, church laity, proprietary security, contractual security professionals, police, and other crime prevention specialists design positive and affirming security approaches for houses of worship. Properly administered crime prevention approaches can enhance the worship experience, rather than detract from it. Security is not limited to big guys, badges, uniforms, and guns. Security encompasses all of the approaches that "U" and "I" contribute to the protection and well being of all worshipers—and you cannot take the "I" and the "U" out of security.

The first thing we need to do is to define *security* and *crime prevention.* Both of these are good terms, but probably mean different things to different people, so there is not a "universally accepted definition." "Security is a hybrid profession blending various skills, backgrounds, and preparation."[5] Even security and police professionals have varying perspectives, often because of the unique degree of specialization required in their current assignment. The terms "loss prevention" and the "protection of assets" are frequently used in the private, proprietary, or contractual security fields, usually to describe inventory shrinkage prevention and theft avoidance programs. The following definition of *security* recognizes these variables:

> Security provides those means, active or passive, which serve to protect and preserve an environment that allows for the conduct of activities within the organization or society *without disruption.*[6]

Crime Prevention: Basic Ground Rules

- Stop denying that crime occurs in places of worship.
- Take "ownership" of your facility.
- Stop delegating crime prevention efforts to the police or sheriff's department. Crime prevention is your responsibility!
- Recognize that you can deter crime.
- Stop talking about it and prevent crime at your place or worship.
- Deter! Avoid! Prevent!

The generally accepted working definition for crime prevention is that it *is the anticipation, recognition, and appraisal of a crime risk and initiation of action to remove or reduce it.*[7] It is a practical method for the direct control of crime, involving analyzing criminal attack methods and designing specific actions within the environment of potential victims to reduce criminal opportunities and manage crime risks.[8]

There are many different forms of crime prevention. First, let's compare crime prevention in a store to crime prevention at a church. Both are relatively simple approaches and both contribute toward a *deterrence* goal and a *business* goal. Shopkeepers deter crimes by being observant, vigilant, and friendly. By offering to assist customers, they create a helpful environment while generating a presence that discourages crimes of surreptitious theft. Shoplifters, if surrounded by alert, friendly personnel and security cameras, go elsewhere where the sales personnel are not aware, wary, or vigilant to accomplish their goals.

The same approach may be used in houses of worship. Adult guardians should be aware, alert, and friendly. By assigning volunteer doorkeepers, welcoming committees, umbrella patrols, youth guardians, and parking lot attendants, crime can be prevented. The criminal may or may not have a change of mind or a change of heart, but the scrutiny of your "guardians" and your general membership may be intimidating enough to cause him to go elsewhere to *prey.* The greatest threat to a criminal is being identified. Each observer or service position added to your volunteer staff will decrease the likelihood of crime.

Security and crime prevention considerations should impact virtually every institutional activity. They should be considered in the planning and construction of new facilities, parking lots, landscaping, and lighting systems and should influence daily operations and program scheduling. This includes everything from making bank deposits to the time you schedule your weekly services. This book will address these topics and provide guidance to assist you in your crime prevention planning efforts.

Risk Options

- Deny the risk.
- Ignore the risk.
- Remove the risk.
- Reduce the risk.
- Transfer the risk.

Risk reduction is one important element of a viable crime prevention program. There are four things that you can do with a risk: Risks can be *ignored, removed, reduced, or transferred.*[9] Many people choose to ignore the risks, saying, "it won't happen to me," or "it won't happen at my facility, even though it has occurred at those OTHER worship facilities down the street." They exist in a state of denial and ignore the fact that crime is occurring.

Secondly, you must remove the risk by assessing when crime is more likely to occur and determining how it may occur. For example, if you determine that the doors are not secure, you should improve the locking system or replace the entire doorframe system. Also, you may remove inadequate locks and windows and remove obstacles that block the view from the street. Additionally, you should conduct a security assessment and respond proactively, thereby removing or reducing potential risk.

Third, risk can be reduced. If you determine that a crime is more likely to occur at night, you can schedule worship, events, and activities during daylight hours. Effective lighting at night and increased visibility during the daytime, as well as radio communication systems for your "guardians" can reduce the crime potential at day and night services.

Additionally, you can transfer the risk to other areas. For example, if you install new locks on the front doors, but do nothing to the back doors, you have increased the likelihood of back door penetration. If you have four parking lots and improve the lighting on three of them, but neglect the fourth, you have just increased the likelihood that victims will be targeted in that lot.

Establishing a group security consciousness can also reduce risks. This is accomplished every day in the business world as security, risk management, and asset control programs have curtailed significant losses. Business leaders are convinced that security can help their bottom line because "you can't make money until you stop losing it through internal and external theft." When religious leaders become concerned about security, their crime risk can be lowered considerably as the opportunity for victimization is reduced.

Crime prevention through opportunity reduction, defined as the *anticipation, recognition, and appraisal of a crime risk, and the initiation of some action to remove or reduce it*, is a practical and cost-effective approach to the reduction and containment of criminal activity.[10]

> **Crime Prevention Through Opportunity Reduction**
>
> - Anticipate risk.
> - Recognize risk.
> - Appraise risk.
> - Initiate action to remove or reduce risk.

Taking appropriate security precautions and committing your worship center to a viable crime prevention program is called "target hardening" within the security profession. Target hardening can reduce your chances of becoming a crime victim by 70 percent or more.[11] The primary crime prevention approaches include knowing about crime in your community, observing your environment, and taking appropriate countermeasures. These measures can be used for both the individual and for institutional properties. We will discuss ways in which you can "target harden" your facility and increase your chances of crime avoidance.

The Reality of Crime

Violent crimes are reported daily in the news. Opinion polls indicate that crime is one of the greatest concerns of all Americans, therefore it is often chosen as a campaign theme for political candidates running for local, state, or national offices.

However, crimes at churches, mosques, synagogues, or temples are handled differently. They are rarely mentioned publicly, occasionally even "camouflaged" by religious and community leaders. Our research indicates that religious leaders do not want to disclose that they are (or were) vulnerable and that a crime occurred on their properties. They fear that people will question their beliefs and their ability to distinguish between good and evil. This is particularly relevant in cases involving sexual assault or abuse by a member.

As a result, many religious leaders will not discuss crime when it is committed by one of their members. Some won't even talk about any crime occurring on their premises.[12] "Worshipers might not come here if they knew the number of people mugged in our parking lots, the number of cars stolen here, or the number of purses taken during our services," say some leaders. Even nonviolent crimes like vending machine burglaries are swept under the rug, because leaders realize that the thief is often an "insider." They may decide not to confront the thief and risk alienating family members or other worshipers.

Primary Crime Prevention Approaches

- Learn about crime in your church's neighborhood.
- Observe the surrounding environment.
- Take appropriate countermeasures.

Your Role in Crime Prevention

Every leader has a responsibility to secure their premises. This was an issue during Biblical times as well, and we can learn much from those who came before us. When the Israelites were building and re-building temples, walls, and fortifications, they "watched" for attack, sounded the alarm when attacked, and responded quickly.[13]

Many of the attacks against Israel were military, but often they were criminal, as marauding nomads demanded water rights, took Israeli hostages into slavery, seized assets and food, and generally preyed upon outlying villages. When Nehemiah was rebuilding the walls and the temple at Jerusalem, his enemies *"conspired together to come to fight against Jerusalem and to hinder it."* [14] Nehemiah was responsible for the temple construction project and he reacted appropriately to prevent further crimes by *"setting a watch."* [15]

We must encourage each religious leader to examine the potential for crime and to seek ways in which they can further secure their premises. We never know how many crimes we prevent by the smallest change in our procedures. Therefore, it is imperative that you implement crime prevention programs and procedures to protect your members, protect your property, and to potentially provide a financial incentive as your insurance company may offer rate reductions for your efforts.

How Bad Is the "Religious Facility" Crime Problem?

Co-authors Quarles and Ratliff have studied crime at religious facilities for many years. Unfortunately, state crime statistical units and the Federal Bureau of Investigation's *Uniform Crime Report*, do not tabulate crimes at church into an easily discernable category. At present, religious structures, sanctuaries, and meeting complexes are listed as "businesses" by the federal/state approved crime analysis agencies, so they can't produce a report on "church crimes." Therefore, we do not have a cohesive, practical crime rate or crime volume index. Our studies indicate, however, that church crime is not provincial. It is universal! Houses of worship all over the United States, indeed, all over the world, are being vandalized, burned, and burgled. Rape, robbery, murder, and assault occur with some level of frequency in houses of worship and their properties.

The elder co-author was 57-years-old at the time of the first printing of this book, in 2001. As a child growing up in Jackson, Mississippi, there were only two or three church crimes reported to the police each year. In 1998, there were 43 church burglaries during a single summer. We now have tabulated thousands of accounts of crimes at religious facilities all over the United States. While the media will report a frenzied killing spree when an aggressor comes into church and shoots worshipers, they often do not report the nonviolent crimes. Our research has focused on both violent and nonviolent crimes at worship centers.

One of the best data sources on crimes against the Jewish Community and its institutions comes from the Anti-Defamation League of B'nai Brith. They provide annual reports concerning the number of hate crimes occurring in a given year. However, they do not track traditional crimes committed at synagogues and religious sites, so robbery, murder, and rape are not statistically targeted in their reports, although vandalism of worship centers and desecration in cemeteries are tabulated as anti-Semitic crimes.

This book will provide many accounts of church crime and will offer many suggestions on ways to prevent crime and to increase your awareness level of the potential for victimization. If we can prevent one victimization, then our work will not be in vain.

Endnotes

1. The Anti-Defamation League of B'nai Brith, *Introduction to Security for Community Institutions: A Handbook*, 4th ed. (New York: The Anti-Defamation League, 1999), n.p.

2. Saul Astor, *Loss Prevention: Control and Concepts* (Los Angeles: Security World Publishing Company, 1984), p. 65.

3. Based on the personal experiences of co-author Quarles, who as a young state police criminal investigator was berated for his audacity in bringing a concealed weapon to church even though the state police department policy mandated carrying a gun at all times. Even as a more mature state drug enforcement administrator, many worshipers looked down on this weapon carrier, believing him to be a "cowboy," rather than a professional police officer. These weapons were concealed. They were never taken out from under his suitcoat, but Quarles was frequently asked if they were there, and when he answered affirmatively, he was often castigated by the "anti-gun" and the "sacrilege at church" crowd. Sometimes there was a different approach, however. One young pastor's wife usually sat near him and his family. When asked why, she said, "I know Chester will protect me, and he's the only one here with a gun." Please be aware, however, that we are not recommending weapons carrying as the answer to church crime.

4. Philip P. Purpura, *Securing Houses of Worship: A Community Service Manual for ASIS Chapters,* (Alexandria, Va.: American Society for Industrial Security, 1999), p. 9.

5. Richard S. Post and Arthur A. Kingsbury, *Security Administration: An Introduction to the Protective Services* 4th ed., (Boston: Butterworth-Heinemann Company, 1991), p. 51.

6. Ibid. p. 10.

7. Arthur Kingsbury, "Functions of the Crime Prevention Officer," (Ph.D. Dissertation), (Stafford, England: Home Office Crime Prevention Center, 1976).

8. The National Crime Prevention Institute, *Understanding Crime Prevention* (Boston: Butterworth-Heinemann Company, 1986), p. 7.

9. Richard Clutterbuck, "Managing the Episode" in *Terrorism and Personal Protection,* ed. Brian Jenkins (Boston: Butterworth-Heinemann Company, 1982), p. 232.

10. The National Crime Prevention Institute, *Understanding Crime Prevention* (Boston: Butterworth-Heinemann Company, 1986), p. ix.

11. J.R. Dixon, *Personal Protection and Security* (Chicago: Nelson Hall, 1985), p. 21.

12. Many pastors who had experienced on-site crimes at their complex would not discuss the details, even after being assured that their names and the name of their church would not be identified in print.

13. Neh. 4, Authorized (King James) Version.

14. Neh. 4:8, (AV).

15. Neh. 4:9, (AV).

CHAPTER 2

SECURITY

The Latin adverb *securus*[1] is the root word from which we get the English term security. The original definition for *securus* was "free from danger." Over the years this definition has included a focus on *protection, shielding, guarding against, rendering safe, and taking effective precautions against.*[2] Post and Kingsbury also state "Security provides those means, active or passive, which serve to protect and preserve an environment that allows for the conduct of activities within the organization or society without interruption."[3] The original translations of the word *securus* included nine basic characteristics. Some of these characteristics emphasized the social aspect of living, but the primary basis for this approach was for personal and family protection.

Primitive man banded together with other families. They used the terrain for crime avoidance advantage. Caves, cliff dwellings, buildings over water, the erection of fortresses and barrier walls were all used to good defensive advantage. Doors, gates, and moats were also early security practices. Later, as towns became more prevalent, other security devices and products came to be used. Even the steeple on the local church synagogue or cathedral was a security tower as guardians watched for enemies. The church bell alerted local citizens to every security issue from fire, storm, or criminal attack.

> **Nine Characteristics of Securus***
>
> 1. Safe.
> 2. Free from danger.
> 3. Feeling no apprehension.
> 4. Protected from danger.
> 5. Providing guardianship.
> 6. Free from risk.
> 7. Satisfying.
> 8. Protective.
> 9. Taking effective precautions.
>
> (*See Post and Kingsbury, p. 3.)

Castles, moats, drawbridges, and security walls, including the Great Wall of China, were constructed for security and protection. The Romans built straight roads to ensure that they could quickly respond to insurrection. Early man joined groups and formed security pacts. These formal or informal contractual relationships helped protect them from marauders and thieves. In banding together as farmers, merchants, and craftsmen within security organizations, each became safer, as his neighbor became his guardian and he theirs. Modern man often looks in askance at old farming communities as they wonder why the farmers didn't live on their farms? Why did they live in village homes and make a slow daily pilgrimage on horseback or on foot to their land every day? Criminologists will tell you that many of those decisions were based primarily on security responses.

Are Churches, Mosques, Synagogues, and Temples Vulnerable?

The answer is "yes," a resounding "yes!" Extremely vulnerable! As we witness the moral decay in America, we realize that many people no longer consider religious facilities sacred. The proliferation of drugs, gangs, and violence shows us that houses of worship are at risk. The fact that our facilities are open and that congregation members and visitors do not expect to be victimized, offers a great opportunity for the criminal.

In fact, the religious facility may be more vulnerable than surrounding homes or businesses. One reason is that many churches are casual about crime prevention. Another reason is that some churches minister to those in need, the homeless, drug abusers, crack addicts, and gang members. Religious facilities have always been vulnerable to the traditional criminals: arsonists, thieves, burglars, robbers, con artists, rapists, and child molesters.

The appearance of the steeple and belfry, big doors, and stained glass windows reflects an appearance of safety. However, the impression of safety may be the very thing that leads to more victimization. People are more at risk when they feel the safest. If you walk down a deserted, poorly lighted area of your downtown, you are wary, vigilant, and prepared to respond to attack. At church, however, your vigilance may subside, placing you at more risk. When the building is empty and the doors are open, the variable of the unknown is increased tremendously. You may not know if someone is hiding in an empty room or if someone is waiting around the corner to turn the lights out and attack you.

Crime Opportunity Model

- A motivated offender.
- A suitable target or victim.
- The absence of guardians.

Houses of worship are vulnerable because leaders refuse to acknowledge the risk and don't take precautions to avoid, deter, or prevent crime to the facility or the worshiper. We encourage you to try this simple test. Look out your entry door. If your building is nestled within a housing or business community, look at their doors. Do you see many security doors, burglar bars, or signs indicating burglar alarms? If so, why doesn't your congregation install these security devices or apply these security approaches? If you see these things in your neighborhood, it is a good indication that you need to revisit your crime prevention program, or develop one quickly.

Do most local apartment complexes use night watchmen, daytime security officers, or other security services? Are your local schools surrounded by chain-link fences topped off with razor wire? Do most of your local businesses have impressive arrays of security lighting? These questions are important because the responses clearly indicate some of the security precautions you need to consider for your facility.

Another consideration is the amount of time that your facility is used. If your facility is used only or primarily during the weekend, there may be a need for more weekday security efforts. If your schedule includes daytime activities, and your complex is left vacant at night, then perhaps you need to protect the facility during the nighttime hours. Additionally, if the building is left open a majority of the time during the day because of day care, schools, or your office-hour regimen, you will need to consider the potential of intruders entering your facility. Considering your schedule is a key factor in a carefully devised quality crime prevention program.

> Crime prevention is an elegantly simple and direct approach that protects the potential victim from criminal attack by anticipating the possibility of attack and eliminating or reducing the opportunity for it to occur—and the possibility for personal harm or property loss should it occur.[4]

When designing your crime prevention program, you must distinguish between easy and difficult targets. An easy target is called a *soft target*. A good example of a soft target would be a purse left in an unoccupied choir practice area. A difficult target is called a *hard target*. By removing the offering or the sacred scrolls or placing them in more secure areas, you are making it more difficult for an offender to succeed. *Target hardening* is

Crime Prevention Approaches

- Anticipate crime risk.
- Recognize crime risk.
- Appraise crime risk.
- Take actions to remove or reduce risk.

the approach used by security and police professionals to deter crime and criminals. It includes installing alarms, lights, locks, doors, fences, and closed circuit television units as well as the use of guard services or police personnel. By hardening crime targets, we deter crime and ensure that we are not soft, easy crime targets.

In developing your security program, it is imperative that you plan well. We encourage you to consult with police and security professionals. Listen to their advice carefully and then decide what is most appropriate for your circumstances and budget. We encourage you to proceed with a vigorous anti-crime program to ensure the safety of all. Learn all you can about the community in which your church is located. Learn about the criminal activity in your community. When does it occur? Where does it occur? At what time(s) does it occur? Who is committing this crime, or what groups are committing the crime? Gangs, drug pushers, prostitution networks, and receivers of stolen merchandise all operate in unique ways. When you have a good understanding of the criminal environment, you can take the steps you need to deter crime. Criminals will not change their lifestyles; however, they may decide to target another area if the likelihood of being seen, recognized, or arrested is too great.

The Four Elements of Every Crime

The Four Elements Of Crime

1. The act itself.
2. The criminal.
3. The victim.
4. The place.

It seems to be oversimplified, but if you focus on the absolute basics, each crime has four elements. There is the crime—any act made punishable by law. Then there is the criminal, the victim, and the place. It is possible, but difficult to alter habitual behavior, so the predators have the advantage over compliant people who are not observant. These people become victims! It is your goal to implement crime prevention strategies to keep your facility from being "the place." You can reduce the likelihood of a criminal act occurring at or near your properties by applying the security principles we are recommending throughout this book, and doing the right things at the right time.

Crime Prevention Through Environmental Design

Crime Prevention Through Environmental Design, called by its acronym CPTED (pronounced sept-ted) encourages the concept of natural surveillance, access control and territoriality.[5] The concept of crime prevention at a particular location is often called "environmental" security, in which properties are designed for crime avoidance, deterrence, and prevention. The environment represents the most delicate and sensitive area of any security program.

An *ethereal* effect, or atmosphere, within the limits of organizational goals and philosophies, must be developed and maintained by the security program. The activities, structure, and management policies of the organization determine the environment within which the organization wishes security to be maintained.[6]

The crime deterrent approach of "place or environment" creates concerns for the offender. These include:

- Access to the offender's target is made impossible, or too difficult and too time consuming.

- Elimination of places where the criminal could conceal his or her presence, making the likelihood of detection or exposure when on the premises too great.

- Arrival of the police or security officers likely when the offender is still on the premises.

- Successful escape is improbable because of poor escape routes and probable police interception.

- Increased likelihood that the offender will be identified through increased observation opportunities.[7]

Timothy Crowe, the author of *Crime Prevention Through Environmental Design: Applications of Architectural Design and Space Management Concepts*, had this to say:

> The physical environment can be manipulated to evoke feelings of personal fear or safety in the users. The same factors or environmental cues that signal safety to a user, tell a criminal that the area is not safe for committing a crime. It is also possible to adapt normal and natural uses of the environment to accomplish the same effects of artificial or mechanical hardening and surveillance.[8]

CPTED has two primary approaches, one active and the other passive. Active approaches include patrols, the use of CCTV, alarms, and parking lot intercoms. Passive design features include lighting, shrubbery, and natural surveillance, which allow individuals to view the exterior of the facility from office and classroom windows overlooking the church parking lot. It also allows law enforcement officers and neighbors to see inside the facility during the event of a robbery or another criminal act. This approach is often used in gas stations and 24-hour curbside stores. Storeowners are encouraged not to block the windows with signs, banners, or merchandise because police officers need to see inside.

On the inside, curtains or blinds should not cover windows because they impede or eliminate surveillance. When bright sunlight is a problem, tinted windows can be used. If venetian blinds must be used, they should not be totally closed. In other words, you should be able to see through the slats. The windows and doors should be clearly visible. The outside of the building should also be adequately lighted.

Natural surveillance gives parking lot patrons plenty of visibility in the space between them and the building because it offers a 360-degree view. There are no blind spots, cul de sacs, or traps in which predators can hide. With natural surveillance the parking patron can see a risk approaching in time to respond, avoid, or leave. A parking lot designed without natural surveillance increases the risk of crime, all crime, both against property and persons.

Flat parking lots are often an advantage versus the tiered lots cut into hillsides and slopes. An "open" parking lot extends the church members' ability to see a reasonable distance. Openness maximizes crime prevention. If you are planning a new parking lot or are going to resurface or retrofit an old one, you will want to view the entire lot from select locations. An ideal lot enables everyone to see the entire lot from all locations. This is critical for your security officers, your welcome committee, and for members and guests. If you have a large parking area, you may need to construct a guard tower similar to those used at many shopping malls and universities. These towers don't need to be gargantuan, usually the viewing platform is only five to eight feet off the ground, but they give the security officer exceptional visibility over an extended area, reducing criminal opportunity. You can also consider using officers on foot patrol, bikes, golf carts, or on horseback before, during, and after services. These professionals can provide guidance or directions to visitors.

If you are planning to construct a parking garage, it should be carefully designed to limit superstructure obstructions and excessive columns and tiers. If you must build a parking garage, ensure that your architect is trained in CPTED, and plan to purchase security cameras and install remote screens in your security room.

An architect trained in CPTED will take special precautions with elevators, stairways, and parking garages. He will minimize any location where a criminal might hide. He will try to increase your natural surveillance options, making you safer and the predators uncomfortable.

CPTED reduces or eliminates exterior hiding spaces for predators by creating what are called "defensible space" zones. Defensible space is "safe" space, and this is how the space at and around houses of worship should be perceived, comfortable for the worshiper and visitor, uncomfortable for the predator.

We encourage the use of "active security" which includes patrols, closed circuit TV (CCTV), alarm systems, and parking lot intercoms. The security patrols, welcome committees, parking lot attendants, and CCTV technology assists in surveying the parking lots for cars, people, or anything out of the ordinary.

Crime Prevention Through Environmental Design
• Natural surveillance. • Access control. • Territoriality.

Parking Lot Lighting

Lighting is generally considered the most important nighttime security resource. If you decide your church needs more lighting, solicit expert advice to ensure that your lighting is evenly distributed and that all "blind" spots are illuminated. A soft, uniform light, free of glare and consistent in its intensity over your parking lot and the entry/exit areas will reduce the potential for crime. A crime prevention specialist, using a digital light meter to measure lighting, will show you which areas have an acceptable or unacceptable lighting variance.

It is important to understand that flooding an area with light can also increase certain types of crime, just as street crimes are deterred with appropriate lighting. If the glare from the lights creates blind spots, these are the locations where predators will take advantage. A light is like a security fence. A fence can keep intruders out, but it can also trap its victims. Just as fences can be used inappropriately, lights can be unacceptable as well. The light must always be uniform. There should not be areas where the lights are very bright and others where it is fairly dark. Lighting variance is a disadvantage, particularly for the elderly.

The Four D's of Crime Prevention

As we show you how to secure your premises from the property line to your buildings, we will promote the "layered" security approach. We asked you to consider access control at the property line and in your parking lots.

You can prevent most crimes by following the "Four D's" of crime prevention. The first step is to deny casual entrance to predators by locking doors and denying them entrance onto the property. The second step to prevent crime is to deter any attack by environmental security or by a manned security presence. The third step is to delay both the entrance and the exit of predators by security hardware and

The Four D's of Crime Prevention
1. Deny entrance. 2. Deter attack. 3. Delay entry/exit. 4. Detect intrusion.

environmental security design or security programs. The fourth step is to increase the likelihood that the crime will be detected, preferably while the offender is still at the scene.

The Four Stages of Every Crime

1. Surveillance.
2. Invitation.
3. Confrontation.
4. Assault.

The Four Stages of Every Crime

Every crime has four stages. Some stages are spontaneous, but others take place over extended periods of time. These stages take place between predators and victims and criminals and buildings. The first stage is called surveillance. The criminal watches the potential victim or the building he intends to attack. Sometimes this lasts for weeks, or even months. On other occasions, it is almost spontaneous. He wants to see who or what he can attack successfully. Increasingly, the criminals are females and youths, as crime rates spiral both within the gentler gender and the very young.

When a criminal has selected a target for victimization, the invitation is offered to delay or distract the potential target. If the victim makes the mistake of stopping, there will be an inevitable confrontation, with the assault to follow, perhaps along with a robbery or rape. In crimes against persons, a confrontation occurs after the criminal gets the target to stop or slow down. Simple questions are asked to distract the victim: "Excuse me. Do you know what time it is?" or "Can you give me directions to Second Avenue?" After you are distracted and looking at your watch, or pointing towards Second Avenue, he may maul you and disorientate you, as he steals your wallet, watch, and ring.

In a building attack, the invitation is subtler. A window or door is open. In the case of a church crime, the criminal is often invited inside, separates himself from others, then remains in hiding until services are over. The crime is committed later. The criminal may enter as a guest or through soliciting services. When the victim is distracted the criminal act is committed.

The confrontation is the beginning of the harsher aspects of the crime. Whether it is a forced-entry or an invited entry, there is an element of confrontation. After the confrontation, there is an assault on persons or property. In a burglary the confrontation could include kicking the outer entrance door open. The assault would include the theft of property.

We stress the importance of surveillance because the primary weakness of any criminal attack is during the surveillance stage. If surveillance can be spotted, the crime can be deterred. An observant church member can approach visitors, welcoming them to the services. In doing so, eye contact is established and the welcoming member may ask the visitors their names, as well as offer them information about the worship complex or community services. This creates an atmosphere of friendliness—but it will also serve as a crime deterrent to those with less than desirable intentions. Criminals don't want to be recognized, remembered, or identified. An observant member's friendly, helpful approach can lower the crime risks for everyone.

Here is an example. Let's say that I am an usher standing on the front step of my church, waiting to open doors and hand out bulletins. I see a couple of people who seem out of place across the street. Two or more ushers could approach them in a non-confrontational way and ask them if they have any spiritual needs. If they were looking for financial aid, you can refer them to the appropriate service agency. If they are considering attending, you can invite them inside, if you decide that it is appropriate during your interview. If they intend to commit a crime at your site, your attention will make them extremely uncomfortable. They will probably leave— never to return. If they are interested in spiritual truths, you have the opportunity to serve and to invite them into your services.

Security Is Your Responsibility

In developed countries, many of us have been subliminally influenced to believe that it is the police department's responsibility to protect us from crime because police and other public safety personnel are given this role. However, we know that individuals must take precautions. We have taken various steps to secure our homes, cars, and businesses. Now, we must take precautions to secure our houses of worship. We must be involved in our own personal security—or we don't have any security. Crime prevention for houses of worship requires an effort from all members of the congregation and a well-implemented crime fighting program.

Philip Purpura, CPP, in writing about church crimes for the American Society for Industrial Security (ASIS) says:

> Limited public police resources hamper a balanced response to arson and other crimes committed against houses of worship. Police response is *primarily reactive*, and departments are under great pressure to solve crimes. As a result, the proactive efforts that would reduce risks at houses of worship are rarely in place.[9]

Believing that "the police are in charge of crime control," detracts from individual responsibility because personal, family, and worship security can never be fully delegated. Depending on police to apprehend all criminals is unrealistic. Depending on prosecutors or judges is inappropriate. The control and management of crime cannot occur through the efforts of criminal justice professionals alone.[10]

Ira Lipman, president of Guardsmark, the nation's third largest private security firm, says, "We can't expect somebody else to take care of our security needs for us. We must handle them ourselves."[11] Good security is the answer to a corrupt world full of predators. Good security is a positive approach to the negative we call crime. If you understand that almost all crimes can be prevented, deterred, or avoided, you and your institutions can survive. Your ministry can both survive and thrive even in the most dangerous crime-ridden neighborhoods.

Security Programs for Religious Facilities

Progressive pastors, priests, rabbis, and other denominational leaders are encouraging reasonable security precautions. Many congregations now have active "security committees" in which members watch the parking lot, buildings, restrooms, and offices during the services. This committee welcomes visitors, but also tries to observe suspicious behavior. Some have implemented a restroom policy in which adults and children are accompanied to the restroom.

Other types of security measures include uniformed or plainclothes security officers. Police officers are increasingly asked to bring their weapons to worship services. Other facilities choose to employ unarmed or armed contractual security guards. Another option is to install a security camera system with the monitors located in the "sanctuary sound booth." The cameras are visible and can be seen by thieves and other predators, thereby deterring the crime. The cameras also allow constant surveillance, reducing the potential for the individual to enter the property unnoticed.

There are many options available that are not costly—in fact, they are free. Contact your local police department or sheriff's office and request a crime prevention assessment at your site. Most crime prevention officers have received nonreactive crime deterrence training. Also, be sure to invite "your officer" or "your deputy" as well, because he or she may have additional information on crime problems in your community. This assessment will provide numerous recommendations to strengthen your crime prevention efforts.

A church security or safety committee is a no-cost option. The committee should discuss the recommendations of the crime prevention officer, the consulting professionals, and security vendors to determine what is best for your facility. Security vendors will focus on primary security equipment such as locks, lights, security hardware, security policies, and security procedures. The committee should also discuss how the church officers and staff handle offering monies and should review the placement and the quality of the safe. The committee should role-play, using "think like a thief" approaches. Committee members should also meet at night and walk around the buildings and parking lots to ensure that the lights are all working and the light quality and intensity is acceptable.

Additionally, the committee should examine the interior and the exterior of all buildings, windows, and doorways to identify security weaknesses. The committee should develop policies relating to locking procedures, key control, and lighting. Perhaps the hours your facility will be open should be reassessed. Based on its assessment, the committee should develop a simple, straightforward plan to address each area of concern.

Security issues should relate to building size, the number of worshipers and visitors on premises, the types of services offered, the age of those attending these services, and the type of community in which the church is located. There are security variables between rural and inner city; between high crime areas and low crime rate areas. Facilities with schools and day-care programs have more concerns about sexual predators, kidnappers, and parental abductors.

Smaller facilities have additional security concerns because the lower attendance level may increase crime and there are fewer witnesses if a crime does occur. Larger facilities may entice predators because there are more monies and valuables accessible during any service. Regardless of the size of the facility, it is necessary to ensure that all doors and ground-floor windows are checked and locked before leaving the premises and that they are checked again when you return to the premises. This security audit can give you assurance that no one entered the building while you were away.

Another no-cost option is a simple "people-friendly" program. A welcoming committee on duty serves at key entryways greeting visitors and members. This assures a personal contact with everyone who walks into your facility. It also sends a subliminal message to criminals: "We saw you. We greeted you. We can identify you." In dangerous, crime-ridden areas, the greeters should be equipped with cellular phones, preset to dial 911 immediately.

Security and safety are issues that, if not implemented properly, can create disunity and division because they alter the way your congregation does business. However, crime prevention strategies can be implemented smoothly and professionally, with little impact on the congregation. If you don't plan for the crime prevention program, it will most certainly be divisive and disruptive. Many of our recommendations can occur with little change and without disrupting your regular method of worship. Properly planned and effectively implemented, a well-designed security program can bring the congregation together in a safer and more secure worship experience.

Endnotes

1. Richard S. Post and Arthur A. Kingsbury, *Security Administration: An Introduction to the Protective Services,* 4th ed. (Boston: Butterworth-Heinemann Company, 1991), p. 3.

2. Ibid.

3. Richard S. Post and Arthur A. Kingsbury, *Security Administration: An Introduction to the Protective Services,* 4th ed. (Boston: Butterworth-Heinemann Company, 1991), p. 30.

4. National Crime Prevention Institute, *Understanding Crime Prevention* (Boston: Butterworth-Heinemann Company, 1986), p.1.

5. Richard S. Post and Arthur A. Kingsbury, *Security Administration: An Introduction to the Protective Services,* 4th ed. (Boston: Butterworth-Heinemann Company, 1991), p. 30.

6. Richard S. Post and Arthur A. Kingsbury, *Security Administration: An Introduction to the Protective Services,* 4th ed. (Boston: Butterworth-Heinemann Company, 1991), p. 11.

7. Robert L. O'Block, *Security and Crime Prevention*, 2nd ed. (Boston: Butterworth-Heinemann Company, 1991), p. 303.

8. Timothy Crowe, *Crime Prevention Through Environmental Design: Applications of Architectural Design and Space Management Concepts* (Boston: Butterworth-Heineman Company, 1991), p. 20.

9. Phillip P. Purpura, *Securing Houses of Worship: A Community Service Manual for ASIS Chapters* (Alexandria, Va.: American Society for Industrial Security, 1999), p. 10.

10. National Crime Prevention Institute, *Understanding Crime Prevention* (Boston: Butterworth-Heinemann Company, 1986), p. xii.

11. Ira A. Lipman, *How to Protect Yourself From Crime* (New York: Avon Books, 1981), p. xxiv.

Part II:
Protecting Property

CHAPTER 3

SECURITY AND CRIME PREVENTION PLANNING

"Planning is required since it is an approach that recommends identifying and stopping a problem before it occurs, of reducing hazards in given situations, and of forecasting rather than reacting to circumstances."[1]

To reduce the opportunities for predators or casual offenders, you must take preventative action. This will reduce the risk of crime and minimize the consequences or loss, should an attack occur. Stopping a crime before it occurs is always the primary goal. The practice of crime prevention is much more than simply applying basic deterrence and avoidance techniques to a problem once it is discovered. It is during the planning stage that most preventative approaches are designed. This is perhaps the most important phase of all.

Form a Security Committee

The security committee should include many members, male and female, young and old, active and inactive. In all probability, the chairperson will be the person who formed the committee, but it is essential that the chairperson be properly motivated and convinced of the importance of this committee and its function. It is the goal of the chair to have as many perspectives as possible when developing security procedures. It is highly recommended that you include members from the law enforcement and security community if these professions are represented within your congregation. If not, we would encourage that you call your local law enforcement agency and ask if they would send a consultant to selected meetings. We would also encourage you to include individuals with various levels of education to again broaden the committee's perspective.

The size of the committee should be representative of your congregation, including age and gender demographics. If you decide to form numerous subcommittees in the planning effort, you will need many volunteers.

Develop a Security Mission Statement

It is important for the security committee to develop a mission statement that clearly defines the goal and objectives of the committee. The security mission statement may be different from the mission statement of the facility because the security committee is more narrowly defined.

After developing the mission statement, it is recommended that you develop "action points" and develop a timeframe for completion. It is at this stage that you may appoint subcommittees in order to accomplish more within a shorter timeframe.

Basic Needs Assessment Questions

- Is our building located in a high or a low crime rate area?
- What are our most vulnerable areas?
- What are our most valuable assets?
- Where are our most valuable assets?
- Who has access to these assets?
- Do we have adequate insurance?
- Do we have an up-to-date inventory list of all our assets?
- If someone was going to rob our facility, when would be the best time, and why?
- Do we have fraud prevention checks and balances in place?
- What types of crimes have occurred at other institutions in our community?
- If someone disrupted our services, how would we handle it?
- If a hostage were taken, what would we do?
- Are we taking precautions in our hiring process?
- Do we have members trained to handle a life threatening or a medical emergency?
- If someone reported a sexual molestation in our congregation, how would we respond?
- Do we need equipment (such as Closed Circuit Television Cameras) to prevent criminal activity at our facility?

Conduct a Needs Assessment

A needs assessment should be conducted by the security committee, with advice and council from the local police and respected private security contractors. The first step is to "brainstorm" to determine what needs to be accomplished. Ask basic questions such as those listed in the Basic Needs Assessment table.

These are just a few questions to generate discussion on the committee and to give some general directives. Security is more than guns and badges and it requires more than just a written procedure. It requires that each person participate and make conscious decisions in view of a "criminological perspective."

Ask for Police Assistance

We strongly encourage partnerships with your local law enforcement officials. For several years, law enforcement agencies across the country have been implementing "Community Oriented Policing," which encourages community partnership representatives to solve problems related to crime. As a proactive approach to reducing crime, law enforcement is generally supportive of these types of projects.

An informal security assessment is simply a walk-through in which officers identify weak spots. Weak spots are areas that are hard to view or areas that are vulnerable. A formal security assessment is a walk-through conducted by an officer trained in Crime Prevention Through Environmental Design (CPTED) who can provide more technical expertise. He will focus on weak spots, but will also provide architectural recommendations to enhance the safety of your facility. If your local law enforcement agency does not have someone certified in CPTED, your state patrol department may be able to help.

By conducting a walk-through, the officers will identify potential hiding places by pointing out areas that are not visible to others or may not be covered by the cameras. They can examine door and window locks and advise if they are sufficient. They can assess the area where you count and/or store the offerings. They can advise if you need to install additional security mechanisms.

Develop a List of Your More Vulnerable Sites

While reviewing the interior of your facility, answer the basic question: Does your worship center have areas that are more likely to be "hot spot?" Listed in the table are some keys to help you determine interior "hot spots."

The exterior would include basic questions such as those in the following table:

Interior "Hot Spots"

- Areas that are not visible by others or are not accessed by others.
- Areas that are not well lighted.
- Areas that are not covered by the security cameras.
- Areas that are small in which a victim would have difficulty escaping.
- Areas in which screams would not be heard.
- Areas likely to be entered by women versus men.

Exterior Questions

- Can the criminals escape quickly from your parking lot and vehicular access areas?
- Can police officers see your premises clearly from the street?
- Do trees and scrubs obscure the view of passersby and patrol officers?
- Are there areas where predators can hide and attack suddenly?
- Does your membership walk to their cars in the dark?
- Is your nighttime illumination sufficient?

While this is not a conclusive list, it will generate much discussion and will help you to focus on situations and events that will be unique to your facility.

Determine When Crimes Are Most Likely to Occur in Your Community

When is an attack most likely to happen? The answer will depend on the type of attack. For example, robberies are more likely to occur at night and with smaller groups. Burglaries are more likely to occur after the Saturday or Sunday evening services. Rape is more likely to occur during the week when the facility is virtually empty. Murder can happen at any time, depending on the motive of the murderer. For example, if someone is out to kill his or her spouse, he or she will often attack during a service. If someone wants to harm the minister, the attacker will more than likely choose a time with few witnesses. Vandalism is more likely to occur at night. Purses and offerings are more likely to be stolen during Sunday morning services.

If your facility is open during the week and you have staff on-site, those staff members are extremely vulnerable to rape, murder, robbery, and burglary at any time. There is safety in numbers and with only a few staff on-site the potential for victimization is greater.

Key Security Actions

- Greeting and observing visitors.
- Securing and locking the doors.
- Tripping the alarm system.
- Tripping the camera/ recorder systems.
- Calling the police.
- Alerting security officers.
- Keeping calm.
- Preserving a crime scene, i.e., not touching anything that the perpetrator has touched.

Develop a Security Plan

This section will identify key players who will be responsible for key actions during regularly scheduled events. The same actions should also be accomplished during nonscheduled events. Only the "key players" will alternate these responsibilities. Key actions would include, but are not limited to the actions noted under "Key Security Actions." There should also be an alternate plan to identify individual responsibility for incidents occurring during your less busy hours. These personnel and actions will be defined according to your needs and schedules. For example, if your facility includes a day care operation, a school, or a soup kitchen, it will be necessary to determine when there are few staff members available and when your operations are more likely to be victimized. One key to always consider is the amount of cash kept on-site. If a theft occurs during your less-busy hours, it is also important to respond appropriately, just as you would during worship services.

Profile of Perpetrators

While you cannot predict who will be a perpetrator of crime in a house of worship, our research indicates that an individual's behavior is a key to determining who might be in your house of worship just to commit a crime.

Security Committee Training

It is important to train your security committee in the security policy and teach them how to respond. It is important that each member knows the "key actions" and has a clear understanding of what his or her duties are.

"Up Front Participants"

These are security volunteers who sit in the front of the building (looking out into the audience) and are in a key position to observe those who enter the building. It is important that they develop a procedure so that they can signal individuals in the audience to "sit up" and take notice if they perceive a threat. The same would apply to security volunteers sitting in the balcony. It is also recommended that individuals trained in security have key seats by the doors, alarms, phones, etc.

Suspicious Behavior

- Individual appears to be nervous and looking around.
- Individual has on inappropriate clothing, such as baggy clothes or big coats.
- Individual is carrying bags or large purses.
- Individual is not focusing on the service and does not participate in activities.
- Individual leaves the service to wander throughout the facility.
- Individual leaves the service after just a brief encounter.
- Individual is not friendly.
- Individual does not make eye contact (may wear sunglasses).
- Individual is found wandering throughout the building and has a weak excuse as to why he or she is there (looking for the rest rooms, etc.).
- Individual appears to be angry.

Interior Facility Policies

Project Identification and Inventory Listing

It is recommended that you make a list of everything that is in the building. Items to include are musical instruments, furniture, office equipment, kitchen appliances, sound equipment, etc. Along with this list, attach serial numbers, makes, models, colors, purchase price, etc. Make certain that each item is marked with an identifying number. It is recommended that you have pictures or a video of every room in your facility. These items should be stored off-site or in a safe deposit box.

Doors, Locks, and Windows

Examine each door, lock, and window. Determine if additional locks are needed or if you need to install new locks. There are various locks that can be purchased to strengthen the doors. Also, consider the type of glass in each. Can it be broken? If so, is the opening big enough for someone to crawl through? Window bars are a good deterrent.

Clearly Visible Rooms

It is highly recommended that each classroom have doors with windows or have long, narrow windows along the doorframe so that individuals can see into the room. This is a good defense against abuse claims, both real and false, and makes it more difficult for someone to hold a classroom hostage.

Strategically Placed Cameras

When conducting the interior and exterior security assessment, determine where you need cameras. Set priorities and strive to accomplish them. It may be admirable to have a camera in each parking lot, but it may be more important to put a camera on the safe, first. This information should be guarded as confidential.

Develop Check and Cash Processing Standards

Review the procedures and determine who has access to the money. When is the money counted? How many people are present? Would a robbery be likely? Is the money counted the same time each week? Would it be a worthwhile investment to have security guards deposit the money with a member? How much money is kept on-site overnight? Is there a way to avoid keeping money overnight? Is money kept in a safe or a fireproof box? Should a deposit be made after the Sunday morning service? How many people are involved with counting the money?

Security Checks

Members of the security committee should be actively involved in conducting security checks during the services. This would include interior and exterior checks. After a service has started, it is imperative to lock some of the doors to eliminate points of access. It is also important that vacant rooms be checked to ensure that no one is hiding.

Key Inventory

Conduct a key inventory to determine who has keys and to which doors. If you cannot account for all of the keys, it is recommended that you have the locks re-keyed. The offices should have a limited number of keys and they should only be issued to individuals who have a legitimate need. If individuals leave your congregation, they should return the keys. Otherwise, you will be faced with having to re-key.

Access Control

Access control is important with key inventory because it is important to know who has access and to what areas. Some areas of the building will need to be secured for evening services if they are not used, i.e., baptistries, choir lofts, balconies, etc.

Emergency Phones

We recommend that each church have a telephone or at least have access to a cellular phone. The strategic location of the telephone could be instrumental in the event of an emergency.

Exterior Considerations for Policy Development

Lighting and Parking

Observe your building at night. Check to see that each window and door is well lighted. Ensure that the doors are visible to the street. Check the parking lot at night to ensure that each area is well lighted. Review the number of entrances. Is it necessary to have more than one open at all times? Should an entrance be blocked after the main service?

Drive-by Visibility

Drive by the facility at night to check lights and visibility. It is also important that someone check the lights on a regular basis to replace burned out bulbs. Check to make certain that trees or shrubs do not block the view. Also, make certain that buses or vans do not obscure the view.

Security Checks

It is important the members conduct security checks during the service and during the week. Alarm systems reduce this need. A partnership with your local law enforcement agency would be an enhancement in this area. However, it is important that the agency knows whom to contact in the event of suspicious behavior.

Money Procedures

To avoid setting a pattern, it is important that deposits are not made on the same day and time each week. Additionally, it is important to vary the route. When transporting money from the safe to the bank, it is vital to have security. Again, each congregation will determine the amount of precautions necessary. If your facility handles large sums of cash, it may be advantageous to contract with a security company or armored car service to make the deposits.

Natural Disaster Plan

It is recommended that all members be trained on the emergency response plan and that it is published and widely distributed. For example, what do you do in the event of a tornado or storm? In the event of a fire, where are the phones and the fire extinguishers located? Is the church address posted by the phones? If you dial 911 and the operator asks if you are in the country or the city, will the caller know? Where is the safest area away from doors and glass?

The actions of the security committee will be instrumental in keeping the congregation calm. They may also save lives by their actions and proactive approaches.

Medical Response

- Do you have basic medical emergency kits?
- Do you have more advanced medical equipment available?
- If someone gets injured, would you have the necessary equipment to prolong life?
- What if someone faints?
- If someone is suffering from low blood sugar, could you assist?
- How do you remove the injured person without disrupting the service?
- During funerals, do you have medical staff on standby for those that are overcome with grief?
- Do you have a medical treatment area that is safe and free from distractions?

Medical Response Team Plan

A medical response team is necessary. The extent of services will again be determined by the size of your congregation. If you have medical professionals who are members of your congregation, ask if they are willing to volunteer to handle any medical emergencies. You can consider having an ambulance on stand-by in the event of an emergency. The topics listed in the table should be discussed when determining your medical needs.

As with many of the recommendations in this book, the degree to which you respond will be determined by the financial resources and the size of your congregation.

Develop Written Security Procedures

Training is the right thing to do. It will protect your congregation, your staff, and yourself. Training is a strong defense in the threat of lawsuits. If your congregation is prepared as to the necessary precautions, then your liability is greatly reduced. By developing policies and procedures, you are indicating a good faith effort to provide a safe environment for everyone. Addressing issues such as medical needs and natural disasters shows a holistic approach to safety issues.

Procedures You Should Consider for Nurseries, Day Care Centers, and Schools

- Bathroom policies.
- Sick child policies.
- Child transfer authorization.
- Who is authorized to work with the children? What is your screening process?
- What doors are open during the day?
- Who has access to the building?
- Late/early arrivals and departure policies.
- Discipline issues.
- What do you do if a parent reports abuse or inappropriate conduct?
- What do you do if you suspect a child is a victim of abuse?
- If a child is absent, whom do you call and at what point?
- Drug and alcohol policy should be posted.

Include provisions for nurseries, day care centers, schools, and youth camps. These, too, must have policies, procedures, and rules. You need to establish these pol-icies in order to ensure the safety for all and to lower the risk factor for the children.

Youth Camps and Gymnasiums

- "No one plays alone rules."
- Approved adults must be present during all activities.
- Showers and locker room rules.
- Co-ed activities rules.
- Inappropriate behavior should be defined.
- Rules of dress and conduct should be clearly defined and agreed upon.
- Parental consent form must be signed.
- Participant consent to the rules of dress and conduct.
- Drug and alcohol policy should be posted.
- When event is concluded, can young people "hang" outside waiting for a ride?

Extra Curricular Events

Events associated with the congregation should be clearly monitored at all times. If your house of worship is assuming responsibility for safety, consent papers must be signed.

Elderly Programs

Depending on the type of program, determine the amount of information that is necessary. If you are providing transportation to an event, you should have a consent form that includes name, address, medical conditions, and emergency contacts. A copy should accompany the person in charge and another kept on file in your office. It is also recommended that someone with a medical background attend as an escort.

If you provide day care for the elderly, it is important to have several contact numbers, list of medications, addresses, physician phone numbers, insurance plans, etc.

Hiring Procedures

This is probably the most important element of having a secure facility. Many times, members of the congregation victimize individuals for years. Literature has supported the claim that we are most likely to be victimized by people we know. Why is this? We let our guard down and become trusting. We allow people to invade our private space and we are comfortable with the invasion.

We have all rejoiced over new members moving into our area and joining our congregation. We often can't wait to put them in a leadership role thinking that they were "sent" to us. How many times have we stopped to check their background by calling their former pastor or employer? Do we know if they left in good standing? Are they running from an allegation of inappropriate behavior?

Do we hire individuals to work with our children without requiring a police records check? If so, we are setting a dangerous precedent. Also, it is recommended to establish a policy that will allow suspension pending investigation if someone is accused of a major violation.

Pre-employment and Pre-assignment Actions

- Contact previous employers.
- Contact previous minister/priest/rabbi.
- Contact two or three previous board members.
- Submit a police records check.
- Ask for a personal history form.
- Discuss illegal drug or alcohol use policy.
- Require a credit check.

We recommend the following actions for new members or new hires (see table).

If it is a standard policy, you can actually issue an "application" form, both to potential employees and to volunteers working in sensitive positions. All of the actions mentioned in the sidebar aren't necessary in every case. A credit check wouldn't necessarily be required of someone who doesn't handle funds, however, it would be entirely appropriate for the administrator handling the business affairs of your facility or for a secretary who writes all of the checks.

Youth teachers and those who work with children and volunteers dealing with these special groups need to be screened. People don't just suddenly become pedophiles. They probably have a history of preying on children. If you are diligent in your screening process, you may be able to find this out. Checking to ensure that you don't erroneously assign an inappropriate person to an important responsibility or a significant task is imperative. Never sign a contract with an employee prematurely. Submit every hiring recommendation to the congregation's board for approval to limit personal liability.

Media Considerations

What do you do when someone alleges discrimination or abuse? What do you do when someone embezzles money? Do you prosecute or sweep it under the carpet? What do you do if a convicted criminal starts to attend your congregation? What do you do if someone attending your congregation commits a horrendous crime? How do you respond to the media?

If a crime occurs at your facility, determine who will issue statements to the media and in what manner. It is very important that the statements be accurate and calming to portray the congregation in a positive manner. Will you release names and conditions of the victims? Will you do so before their relatives have been contacted? What are the ramifications of releasing the information?

> **Develop a Response Plan for Other Emergencies—Be Prepared**
>
> - Armed robbery.
> - Hostage events.
> - Vandalism.
> - Service disruption.
> - Other serious crimes.
> - Heart attacks and other medical emergencies.
> - Natural disaster.

A clear and concise media policy can protect the congregation from libel, slander, and defamation lawsuits.

Responding to Allegations of Sexual Misconduct or Abuse

What do you do if someone reports that they have been a victim of sexual misconduct or abuse? What is the first "reaction" versus the first "response?" Whom do you call first? What if the allegation is against the person you would call first?

How do you ensure that the victim is telling the truth? Who will conduct the investigation? When it is completed, who will be provided a summary of the results? Do you take precautions to ensure that the victim and perpetrator are separated? How do you implement damage control within the congregation and outside to the community? Should you report the incident to the police department? Should you conduct our own internal investigation first? Should the alleged perpetrator be suspended? These are tough questions that will need to be handled with care. These very issues can destroy a congregation.

Internal Versus External Investigations

It is important to establish a policy as to how to handle situations involving abuse, sexual misconduct, etc. Are we going to investigate the complaint or are we going to call our primary law enforcement agency? If the charges are sustained and the state wants to prosecute, are we going to participate? If we allow someone to resign and move on, are we not condoning their behavior and allowing them to continue their lifestyle? On the other hand, if we participate in a court trial, is the congregation going to suffer from negative press? Will the community accept our decision? How do we keep the behavior of one person from impacting the reputation of the congregation?

Developing a holistic approach to security is more than alarms and locks. We must ensure that our members are secure—secure from physical or spiritual harm, secure from an overly aggressive press, secure from individuals whom they have trusted, and secure from the unknown.

Endnotes

1.   B.M. Gray II, as found in Lawrence J. Fennelly, ed., *Security Applications in Industry and Institutions* (Boston: Butterworth-Heinemann Company, 1992), p. 2.

CHAPTER 4

TRESPASSERS

A beautifully designed church, located on Capitol Street in the capital city of a southern state, was the dominant institution attended by the communities' most affluent residents. As the neighborhoods surrounding it grew older, a community malaise crept in. Instead of winning garden club awards for the most beautiful lawns in the city, residents mowed their lawns less often, parked cars that wouldn't start under their shade trees, and took the garbage out when they felt like it. Weeds replaced the well-designed flowerbeds.

Drug pushers, prostitutes, burglars, thieves, and vandals moved into the neighborhood. Gangs began enlistments from one sub-community to another, some of them violent gun carriers with many members linked to drug trafficking. Local businesses began to install burglar alarms, bars, and steel fences with razor wire wrapped at the apex, and began taking additional crime prevention precautions. Several businesses, successful over many decades, failed in this environment. Lacking community policing, the tax base declined as the more affluent residents moved to other areas, away from the city. The malaise continued, disproportionally and exponentially.

The church was also affected by the change in the neighborhood. The church staff would come in early Sunday morning to see if there was anything to detract from worship. On occasions, it was obvious that there had been a knife fight on the front steps of the sanctuary. Liquid cleansers and high-pressure hoses removed these stains before services. Condoms were found back in the shrubbery, indicating drug trades for sex. It became obvious that the church's front steps were a major drug distribution point.[1] Police intelligence agents confirmed this observation.[2]

One Sunday morning, an 11-year-old girl was startled when she discovered a transient sleeping in her Sunday school room. Waking up, he immediately reassured her by saying, "Don't worry little girl, I won't hurt you." But she responded appropriately by screaming and running away. By the time an adult responded, he was gone. This was not the fervent imagination of a child because the intruder's body odor and the smell of cheap alcohol remained. While he was probably just a harmless transient sleeping off a Saturday night drunk, his attempts to calm the girl indicated that he may have had other intentions. While there are other possibilities, he could have been a nightmare waiting to happen.

The church experienced several other crimes including discovering the body of a murdered teenage girl in a storage building on church property. During services, automobiles were stripped of their sound systems, tires, and accessories. These initial crimes are the "prodromes" (a Greek word meaning *running before*) and the PINs (Pre-Incident Indicators), which are the gauges of past and current crimes. As more and more families left the church because of the criminal activity, ultimately the decision was made to build another facility in another nearby town, rather than continuing work within the community and dealing with these problems. This decision was amicable, but decisions to relocate churches and synagogues over crime issues have often resulted in controversy when members are unwilling to compromise and reach a majority decision.[3]

At Central Presbyterian Church in Jackson, Mississippi, a transient, who had visited the church "welfare" office on previous occasions, murdered an associate pastor. The minister knew him and was comfortable in his presence. This transient was a MICA (Mentally Imbalanced and Chemically Addicted) whom the minister had counseled. On this occasion, however, the man became enraged when the minister did not provide all of the resources he demanded. Central Presbyterian later closed its doors, its members transferring to other local churches.

At Christ United Methodist Church in Memphis, Tennessee, a kidnapped girl, the daughter of a wealthy grocer, was held hostage for many weeks in the church attic. During worship services, she was hidden in the alcove. At night, the transient holding her would come down and steal food from the kitchen. The girl was finally rescued when her abductor was arrested. The food products missing from the kitchen led church leaders to call in the police for a thorough search of the premises. The kidnap victim was a surprise.

These are just a few examples of various types of crimes against religious institutions. The first example showed the impact a declining community had on the church. The second and third examples demonstrate how individuals can trespass and commit other crimes on your properties.

Prodromes and PINs

As previously mentioned, the Greek word "prodrome" (pronounced praudrome) means *running before*. It is an indicator that something is about to happen. In a crime intensive environment, that "happening" is almost always bad. Some criminologists use an imprecise acronym for this prediction component of escalating crime. PINs (Pre-incident Indicators) are used to show that there is a crime spiral and that present crimes and past crimes can be used to predict the probability of future crimes. When crime becomes established as a normative component of daily life, crime actually begins to increase exponentially, feeding upon itself as in a frenzied feast of evil. PINs can also be used to predict crimes against individuals.

Security Basics

Security basics include access control as a major component of any crime prevention, deterrence or avoidance procedure. Good security is developed incrementally. The first security component is access control, so your first goal should be to deny casual access to your building. However, once inside, access control focuses on restricting entry into offices, money-counting rooms, or sites where valuables are stored. An important consideration in access control is to limit the accessibility of children to nonparents. Access control also includes limiting entry to restroom facilities, stairwells, or restricted classrooms.

Parking Lot Access: A Primary Security Issue

The first crime influencing access control issue begins at the exit from your city thoroughfares onto your parking lots. Many access/egress points are efficient in expediting the traffic flow immediately before and after services, but sometimes there can be too many entrances/exits. While we appreciate casual access when we want to drive into the lot, sometimes an excessive number can negatively impact your crime control program.

If you have too many access points, criminals can enter undetected to victimize cars or the worshipers returning to their cars. We encourage large facilities to limit access during services by placing barriers across the entranceways. Some churches actually close off access roads with gates or chains during services, removing them after the services. Another way of restricting access is to allow parking lot or security committee members to park their cars across these access/exit lanes. Of course, you are not going to restrict all lanes because there may be emergencies or late arrivals. However, by restricting the excessive access points, you are making it more difficult for those with criminal intent to enter your premises. We encourage facilities to use uniformed security officers to direct traffic and volunteers to advise visitors on where to park and provide general information.

Restricting access is not the only requirement. You will need to station welcome committee members, umbrella patrols, or security officers at the access/egress routes. Some larger facilities use security carrels, called kiosks, within the security profession. Some kiosks are fabricated over trailer assemblies, so they can be moved conveniently. However, kiosks are usually installed on a semi-permanent foundation and equipped with external lighting, telephone lines, and a facility radio transceiver. Your security officers or welcoming committee can be posted at the kiosk in all types of weather to guide (and guard) visitors and members.

By directing traffic past security officers or the welcoming committee, you are ensuring that visitors and members will be welcomed and assisted with directions, if necessary. This makes worshipers feel welcome and more secure. This makes predators feel uncomfortable. They don't want to be recognized, stopped, investigated, or arrested. Predators see that the on-site people will prevent inappropriate conduct at the parking lots.

A thief entering the lot will be channeled past security officers or a welcoming committee, sometimes even past a CCTV camera recording the thief's picture and that of his car and license plate. Even without the technology there is the potential of being identified. What if someone recognizes him? What if the person at the access/egress choke point writes down the license tag number of his car? The thief may want to burglarize a car, take a tire, or steal a car sound system, but he doesn't want to get caught—so he'll drive down the road to another parking lot where his actions will not be observed.

The choke point is an ideal access-influencing security approach, very inexpensive, yet very effective. The territoriality approach clearly demarcates property lines, showing worshipers and even potential intruders the areas owned and guarded by the church. Territoriality can be influenced by lawns, buildings, fences, gates, and lighting.

What Can Pastors, Rabbis, and Priests Do?

Religious leaders must address the crime issue! Crime doesn't appear on its own—nor does it disappear by chance. Whenever a person-to-person crime has occurred, a security or safety committee should respond immediately. If you do not have a security/safety committee, start one immediately. You can prevent, deter, and mitigate crimes against individuals and institutions. You just need to find a security approach acceptable to your congregation.

The Onion or "Layered" Security Approach

Your security programs should be "layered." Security professionals sometimes refer to this concept as the "onion" approach. It is used by personal protection specialists to protect VIPs and properties. For example, the Secret Service uses this approach when protecting the president of the United States. They have agents in very close, further away, and remote to his location. These are the inner to outer layers. These security professionals are stationed at appropriate locations and are used to assist primary agents who are "watching" for threats and to decrease the likelihood of assassination or kidnapping.

The "layered" security approach is appropriate for your security program, because both people and property are protected. The extremes of your church property are the outer security layer. Usually the parking lot, located at the extreme perimeter of your property, is the outer security "layer." Your security must begin here, at the perimeter.

Layers of Security

- 1st layer: Streets and parking lots traffic officers and parking guardians.
- 2nd layer: Outside and "umbrella" welcome committee are observing walkways and grounds.
- 3rd layer: Building entranceway welcome committee.
- 4th inner layer: Ushers and sanctuary hosts.
- Innermost layer: Controls rostrum access as well as pastoral protection and distinguished speaker personal protection.

The outermost security is usually accomplished by parking attendants, volunteers, members, guardians, security or police officers, and traffic wardens. It is intended that these individuals are conspicuous with their radios and uniforms. Corporal Chip Gillette, the first responding police officer to the 1999 Wedgewood Baptist Church "spree" shooting in Fort Worth, Texas, believes that volunteers should wear distinctively colored vests clearly marked as "welcome committee" or some similar designation.[4]

Those designated can direct traffic and assist in parking lot traffic control while they are watching cars, people, and looking for anything out of the ordinary. The Bellvue Baptist Church in Cordova, Tennessee, is one of the largest churches in the Mid-south. Bellvue has a marked security patrol vehicle, complete with security decals on the doors, emergency flashers, and the standard police/security vehicle "bar" light system, although it is equipped with amber flashers versus the police blue to comply with good policy and Tennessee State Code.

During services, this vehicle is constantly roving to ensure the safety of all worshipers. If the security officer finds someone sitting in a car, he approaches the visitor courteously to see if he can provide assistance. However, at the same time, the parking lot visitor's identity is determined and notes are made about their automobile description and tag number. Legitimate worshipers appreciate this courteous attention while those with less than pure motives will feel uncomfortable and leave. The Bellvue parking lot is much safer than that of the other churches in the area. It is also worshiper friendly. The Bellvue parking lot is an unacceptable environment for those who come to commit crimes against worshipers, to steal cars, or to steal from the unoccupied cars parked there.

The next layer of security should include your outside greeters, standing just outside the entry doors. These individuals may be equipped with portable radios or cellular phones. They open doors for all who enter, paying particular attention to the needs of the elderly or infirm. They give directions to classrooms and can provide aid in many other ways. In inclement weather, they provide umbrellas and help with loading and unloading wheelchairs or baby strollers, if aid is needed.

The next layer in your security circle is the usher or greeter, congregational volunteers who stand immediately inside the building, usually in the foyer outside of the sanctuary. These individuals hand out bulletins, smile, greet, and provide directions. They make members feel wanted, visitors feel welcomed, and criminals feel uncomfortable. The innermost security circle should be in close proximity to your leaders. In one large Protestant church the co-authors visited, police officers sat on the stage with concealed weapons. Because these officers are also members, the average onlooker has no idea that this facility has a well-designed security program. The "onion" approach can work at your facility, too.

Parking Lots

First of all, you must recognize how much wealth is represented in your church parking lot. New cars, classics, hubcaps, tires, motor parts, and articles left inside the car are all up for grabs in an "unmanned" parking lot. The thief can steal the car, take the parts, or break into the car to take valuables. Other predators wait until a victim returns to commit a robbery. Sometimes these crimes escalate into car hijackings, personal kidnappings, rape, and even murder.

We do not have specific crime statistics on parking lot crimes at churches, mosques, and synagogues; however, we can easily extrapolate from commercial crime data. A 1992 National Institute of Justice study determined that "parking facilities represented the third most frequent place in which violent crime (rape, robbery, and assault) occurred in America.[5] During that year alone, some 1,400 violent parking lot crimes were reported every day in America.

During our research, we found numerous accounts of crime in parking lots adjacent to worship facilities. In Winston-Salem, North Carolina, a woman leaving a wedding ceremony was stabbed to death some 12-feet from her car.[6] In Bridgeport, Connecticut, a priest was robbed of his money, a watch, a ring, and a necklace in the church parking lot.[7] In New York City a rabbi was stabbed outside of his synagogue.[8] In Durham, North Carolina, 16 automobile burglaries were reported and numerous cars were vandalized.[9] In New York City, a minister and three members of his congregation were robbed in front of their church after an evening worship service.[10] Again, in New York City, a priest and two members of his parish were critically wounded in a shooting as they stood on the steps of their church. In Crete, Illinois, a church van and building were vandalized.[11] These crimes continue to occur frequently all over the United States.

What If the Onion Approach Doesn't Work?

What do you do if the onion approach doesn't work? For example, the security filter layers fail, letting in a transient. Say you discover a MICA (Mentally Imbalanced and Chemically Addicted) or a person begging for money in your facility. How do you respond? What should you not do? How can you gauge the danger level? Are strangers the only threat? Do you have a working and available telephone? Do you have a panic alarm button? Are there any other personnel available to assist you?

We found numerous examples of violence when religious counselors dealt with divorcing couples, especially when one spouse has been violent toward the other. The aggressor is well aware of the scheduled worship services and may decide to make a move. What if he shows up? What if he shows up drunk? This is a matter of careful evaluation because the place you should stop him is at the entranceway. This is another form of access control. When counseling members, you must ask them about violence and determine if they expect any problems. Granted, sometimes there are no warning signs, but most of the time there have been other indications. We give examples in this book where estranged husbands have shot ministers. In one case, a man drove his pickup truck through the church doors and into the foyer.[12]

Access Control Example

Joseph and Mary Smith were getting a divorce. Both were longtime church members, but Joseph had exhibited a violent temperament and struck Mary repeatedly. She was hospitalized for nine days. The church leaders knew this. Mary still attended church, but Joseph dropped out.

Mary told the pastor that her husband was threatening to kill her. Three weeks before their divorce was final, Joseph shows up at church, drunk, inappropriately attired, and belligerent.

Are your "gatekeepers," going to let him in? I hope not, because the problems could escalate if you do. Would you let him in if he was sober and wearing a suit? That is a matter of careful evaluation as well. The place you stop Joseph, a member of your church, or any other threat, is at the parking lot or doorway.

A simple, basic solution is to lock all of your doors when meetings are not scheduled, thereby limiting casual access to those who have less than honorable intentions. Many facilities want the doors open 24 hours a day. "It is the way it has always been," they say, implying that the facility administrator would commit a grave error if the policy changes. Locking the doors decreases the likelihood that security nightmares have sneaked in and are hiding in your facility.

For example, a transient may enter your church with no intention of further criminal activity. He or she may just want a place to sleep. The trespass is relatively minor and it seems innocent enough. However, you should understand the position of the church secretary who arrives at 8 a.m. and discovers this uninvited guest while she is by herself. There are no restrictions here. She is alone, protected only by the intentions of the transient and her ability to protect herself. This crime could progress from simple trespass to robbery, rape, and even murder.

While we do not want to stereotype all homeless transients as thieves, rapists, or murderers, it is nevertheless true that there is a strong probability that there is violence and crime in their past. If they don't have a place to sleep, chances are they have just been released from jail or prison, or they are no longer welcome in the local homeless shelters. They may be looking for food in your kitchen, or simply a place to rest in inclement weather. However, we can never (or should never) forget that many of these people are on medication, illegal drugs, alcohol, or have a history of violence. Since we do not know their intentions, we must proceed with caution.

At one recent "church security" meeting a pastor shared this account about a young man who began attending his church. Instead of a suit, he wore jeans without socks and a frayed t-shirt. He walked into a packed crowd after the services started and sat on the third pew facing the pastor. His demeanor was so startling that an usher walked down and sat beside him, concerned that he might cause a problem. This was a proactive security response, but was also service oriented.

Instead of confronting him, the usher shook his hand, welcomed him while the congregation was singing, and sat beside him. His behavior was exemplary during that service. The young man returned. This time his behavior was acceptable, but he just didn't "look" right. He had the wild-eyed look of a psychiatric patient or drug abuser. Not knowing what was wrong, the leadership accepted him, welcomed him, and watched him. In future services, ushers would sit on either side, and another was often seated behind him, and occasionally another positioned himself to the visitor's front. In fact, they ushered him to a location where they could more easily influence his behavior, if his actions became unacceptable. The church leadership was appropriately concerned but still they accepted him, welcomed him, and talked to him after services.

After several services, the young man requested church membership. As he was counseled privately, he revealed that he was on probation for drug offenses, that he had rejected a loving family, and lived a life apart from them and all the things that we know as good. Influenced positively in a prison ministry, but still caught up in a post trauma stress disorder, he came to this church for spiritual and emotional healing.

Handled appropriately, this man found a loving group of friends and congregational membership. Handled inappropriately, this scary-looking guy would have never been allowed in the front door. How do you handle it? We can't tell you how to handle every situation. We, personally, have strong reservations about allowing people into your services if they are obviously under the influence of alcohol or drugs. However, street evangelists, religion funded homeless shelters, and Salvation Army personnel couldn't function if they evicted all the drunks. What are the differences between a worshiper, a visitor, an intruder, or trespasser? The following suggestions may help you decide what is right for your congregation.

What Should You Do?

If you enter the building and discover someone is there (and they don't see you), you should leave immediately if you are alone. If you are not alone, you should find another person immediately. Never confront someone by yourself. Depending on the circumstances, it might be appropriate to call your local law enforcement agency and let them handle the situation.

If you encounter someone accidentally, tell them that you are not alone–whether this is totally true or not. This misrepresentation for safety and security is scripturally allowed. In the New Testament, the Apostle Paul misrepresented his travel plans for his own safety, so you can, too. In the Old Testament, the Torah and the other Hebraic Scriptures we have other examples of the misrepresentation of Abraham, Isaac, Moses, and the prophets and leaders of Israel.[13] If you feel the person is dangerous, distract him or her, and flee. There is nothing in the church that they could steal which would mean more than your personal safety.

If you are alone and know that no one is coming, don't let the person know this. Act as if someone is "on the way." Again, your goal is to extricate yourself from the situation as quickly as possible. If you are close to a phone, make a call to another person or to the police. Merely reporting the presence of an intruder to someone else is a strong indicator that he should behave or that he should leave. "Before I can assist you I must let our (pastor, priest, minister, or rabbi) know. It's a policy requirement. Would you mind filling out this visitors card?" Try to take control of the situation.

If you find an "uninvited" guest, talk to him or her. There are certain things that you should notice. For example, if you saw a strange man get out of a car, you could talk to him about his vehicle. How long has he had it? Where did he buy it? Did he put a lot of mileage on it? Or does it have an infant seat? The responses to these questions will give you a lot of information about the person and help you assess the potential for risk.

Questions to Ask Intruders

- Who are they?
- Where are they from?
- Why are they here?
- How long have they been in town?
- Where are they headed?
- Who is expecting them and when?
- How did they enter the building?
- What assistance do they need?
- Are they employed?
- Are they fugitives?
- Are they married?
- Do they have children?
- Where are the wife and children?

If someone says he is hungry, offer to meet him at a local restaurant. Do not ride with him in your car or his car, but drive separately. This is safer. We emphasize that you should not go alone. Ensure that you go to a restaurant that is busy. This increases your safety level. Additionally, you may want to keep gift certificates on hand to give to individuals in need. Don't keep a cash drawer! If someone is requesting rent money, you may offer to meet with the landlord and you can provide referrals to social services. If someone needs gasoline, you may issue a gift certificate or call ahead to a pre-chosen gasoline station and have the amount credited to your church account.

Be cautious if you are asked to give a "tour" of your building(s) or to allow a stranger solitude in the sanctuary. Predators often attempt to distract you while they inventory the valuables in your building. This happens frequently when professional thieves are involved.

When the person leaves you need to write a summary of the event while it is still fresh on your mind. Write down your observations about clothing, facial features, vocabulary, speech patterns, birthmarks, and tattoos. Write down what you remember of your interview and the interests the intruder expressed. If you have formed opinions about language groups, ethnicity, or educational level, record these observations as well. Describe the car and record the license plate tag number. Record this surreptitiously, if possible, and keep this note in your files. This may be invaluable if the person returns or a criminal act is committed on your premises or a facility down the road. Discuss this incident with your security committee and other congregational members who need to be informed. This will ensure that the person hasn't been there before. The conversation will help make others aware and more likely to identify this character in the future.

If someone requesting assistance gives you a name, ask to see his or her driver's license. While this is part of your security program, you may tell them that church policy requires that you make a photocopy for the church file before you consider offering any aid. Granted, you may not be able to spot a fake driver's license or identification card; however, it could help lessen your anxiety to know they at least have one. A sincere person would not hesitate to give it to you. After all, it's required when you test-drive a new car or even when you are shopping for an apartment or home. In some states, it is required that visitors give their driver's license to the real estate agent when they drop in on an "open" house.

We encourage you to establish a security check system after services where two or more members walk through the building, checking doors and windows and ensuring that no one is hiding. Two or more individuals together lower the probability of a criminal attack by 67 percent according to a study conducted by the San Francisco organization, Community United Against Violence.[14] Three or more individuals together lower the chances of criminal victimization by 90 percent.[15] Additionally, upon reentering the building after services, it is recommended that your security team drive around the building noting windows and doors. Once inside, check the areas which are most vulnerable, looking for a forced entry or an intruder.

As a congregation, it is important that you be informed on the social services available in your community. Be able to quickly refer the needy to shelters, housing agencies, medical clinics, food banks, financial assistance for utilities, and clothing, etc. We recommend that you utilize all of the resources in your community as you seek to aid those making benevolent requests. After all, you are paying for them with your tax dollars, and it is inappropriate to duplicate services unnecessarily.

Don't Meet Alone with Unannounced Strangers

Due to the number of documented cases of robbery, assaults, rapes, and murders, we do not encourage pastors, priests, or rabbis to meet one-on-one with strangers. When strangers call, you should explain that they must have an appointment or be willing to come back to meet with you and an associate. That way, you can arrange to have someone else present in the building. This will reduce the potential of being a victim and will reduce the opportunity for the person to suggest that you have acted inappropriately.

In any situation, you must trust your "gut instinct." If you are uncomfortable, terminate the session. Remember, your mission will not be fulfilled if you suffer a tragedy at the hands of an intruder. Your ministry will also be harmed if your reputation is tarnished by scandalous accusations. If you are feeling uncomfortable with the intruder and the situation, then ask them to join you in prayer. (Keep your eyes open—just in case). Your simple prayer with them may be enough to dispel these thoughts and it may enable you to help them.

Many people seek financial, physical, or spiritual assistance. Most are sincere, but to some this request is a guise. Places of worship are a logical place to seek assistance and we realize that it is part of our mission to assist individuals in need; we also do not want to fall victim to someone with less than honorable intentions. We must proceed with caution, because in not doing so we may put our safety and the congregation's safety at risk.

We are not suggesting that anyone who stops by your facility is a murderer or rapist. However, we are suggesting that there may be a fine line between those exhibiting appropriate and inappropriate behavior. Only your observational skills combined with spiritual insights may discern the difference. Meeting the needs of people requiring spiritual and physical assistance is an important challenge. However, being safe is of utmost importance. You can't minister comprehensively in an unsafe environment.

Sometimes the intrusive threat apparently comes from within the religious community. Co-author Quarles had just completed a security analysis and risk assessment of a church in Wisconsin. One week later, the pastor, a seminary graduate on his first assignment, was leaving the church when a van rolled into his parking lot. Replete with ministry symbolism, the van was marked as an out-of-state nondenominational religious organization. The driver got out with a Dale Carnegie smile and approached the pastor. Engaging him in polite conversation, the visitor asked if the pastor and the church could help him. The visitor wanted to preach in his church the following Sunday.

After explaining that he only let representatives of his denomination speak at his church under ordinary circumstances, and then only when he knew them personally so as not to be concerned about doctrinal abuses from the pulpit, the visitor exploded. The pastor went on to explain:

> "He grew angry and told me that I was not a called minister and that I was close-minded like everyone else in this town and that God was going to curse our church because of this." By the end of his berating condemnations he told me that "I was of the devil and that he was going to come to church on Sunday to make sure that the congregation knows their pastor is from Satan."

"I don't know if he will come this Sunday or not—and if he does, my sense is that he will do no more than insult me for a while, and then leave—but in light of school and church shootings, I have called the police to ask their advice."[16]

Thank goodness the "visiting" evangelist didn't return. However, there were many alterations to normal church practices that day and in the following weeks. A fairly small church, the back and side doors were locked after Bible study. A sign was placed on each exterior door asking late-arriving worshipers to enter through the sanctuary entranceway. An extraordinary welcoming committee was in place, which included the pastor who was the only member who could identify the "evangelist." Cellular phones were brought in and the police were apprised of the threat. This church initiated "good" crime prevention techniques. Remember, trespassers and intruders come in all shapes and sizes. Their goals vary. It is often difficult to distinguish between the honorable and those with less than honorable intentions.

Endnotes

1. A private affirmation by a senior pastor in a southern city, affirmed by the crime prevention officer of that jurisdiction.

2. Crime prevention unit of the city police department involved.

3. A quote from a pastor who will remain anonymous. "Preacher, my grandad's funeral was in this church, my daddy's funeral was in this church, my mom's funeral was in this church, and I am not leaving this church unless the walls fall in. I don't care about these other issues. I'm staying."

4. Corporal "Chip" Gillette. Telephone interview with co-author Quarles, 10 January 2001.

5. Captain Robert L. Snow, *Protecting Your Life, Home, and Property. A Cop Shows You How* (New York: Plenum Publishing, 1995), p. 266.

6. J. Graham, "Churches Seek Refuge From Crime, *State* (Columbia: S.C., 7 December, 1992), n.p.

7. M.P. Mayko, "Churches No Longer Safe Havens From Crime," *Connecticut Post* (Bridgeport, Ct., 28 April, 1993), n.p.

8. R. Pierson and F. Dicker, "Rabbi Knifed in Wave of Anti-Jewish Attacks," *New York Post,* 14 December, 1992, n.p.

9. T. Richisin, "Thou Shalt Not Steal Is Ignored: Churches Once Immune to Crime Buy Protection, (Raleigh, N.C. *News and Observer*, 25 February 1993), n.p.

10. D. Saltonstall, "Holy Heist: Once the Safest Havens in the City, Places of Worship Have Become Targets of Choice for Vandals and Thieves," *New York Daily News*, 8 August 1993, p. 18A.

11. T. Tierney, "Vandal Eludes Cops, Upsets Crete Pastor," *Chicago Tribune, 12* December 1994, n.p.

12. An event that took place in California. Told in confidence to Chester Quarles, co-author, by a church official present at the time.

13. 1 Sam. 16:1–2, Gen. 12:12–13, Gen. 20:2, Josh. 2:1–7, 2 Kings 10:18–30, 1 Sam. 20:5–29, Gen. 26:7–11, 1 Sam. 19:11–17, 1 Sam. 20:1–2, Exod. 5:3, Authorized (King James) Version.

14. Michael Castleman, *Crime Free: Stop Your Chances of Being Robbed, Raped, Mugged or Burglarized by 90%* (New York: Simon and Schuster Publishers, 1984), p. 67.

15. Ibid.

16. From a threat registered at a Protestant church in Wisconsin on September 7, 2000. Sources wish to remain anonymous.

CHAPTER 5

BURGLARY

He had a serious expression and in a quiet, somber voice said, "I did it because it was easy. Churches are easy targets…" He continued to explain how he had burglarized several Kentucky churches. The "loot" was easily fenced for "fast cash" and it was a good return based on his investment and risk. The only reason he was incarcerated was because the last church he burglarized had engraved their property with identifying numbers. After he pawned the valuables, the police department tracked the numbers to the church and placed him under arrest. Without the precautionary steps taken by a church administrator, he might have continued on his burglary spree.

In a Mesa (Ariz.) Tribune article[1] the Reverend Richard Kaeske of the St. Mark's Evangelical Lutheran Church of Mesa, Arizona, tells how he discovered that his church was burglarized again. After 11 burglaries in his 26-year ministry, he said that he is tired of the hassles. He wishes that the burglars would walk through the front door and ask for what they need because he would gladly give it to them.

Some burglars prey almost completely on churches. Reporters Kiran Crowley and Erica Browne reported in the New York Post that a church organist from Manhattan had looted more than 500 churches over the last decade.[2] He traveled from state to state and was easily hired as an organist. He was very talented and played the organ, piano, and harpsichord. While doing so, he learned the building layout and the procedures for offering disposal. Some of these churches had very expensive items made of or overlaid with precious metals. He stole these exclusively, having a particular source through which to sell these items. In one month, the organist netted over $40,000 in stolen goods. While all denominations do not use precious metals on religious artifacts, nevertheless, you should take special care in checking the background of individuals you hire whether as temporary or part-time employees.

Churches, mosques, synagogues, and temples have been burglarized in every state and in foreign lands. Rural churches and urban churches have been victimized. Poor boxes, food items, clothing, purses, pianos, and other items have been stolen. Chalices and Torahs have been taken. Statutes of the saints and the Virgin Mary have been stolen while others have been desecrated and destroyed.

Why would someone choose to burglarize a church? First, let's consider the very obvious. Houses of worship are vacant more hours than not. The burglar can pick morning, afternoon, evening, or nighttime. Because worshipers and members come and go with regularity, the thief can maintain surveillance and plan for the best attack alternatives. He wants to enter quietly and leave quickly, with a significant financial return for his risk. A professional thief makes a choice to avoid confrontation if at all possible. If there are no witnesses, his chance of success is tripled.

Secondly, in addition to being vacant, religious institutions are targeted because of the low risk. If a burglar decides to enter a building in the daytime and encounters someone inside, he can usually escape without notice by inquiring about services or asking for directions. While inside, he has the opportunity to take inventory and can decide if he needs to return. Additionally, religious facilities are often surrounded by large parking lots instead of immediate neighbors. If they have neighbors, most neighbors would not notice a truck or car parked in the parking lot. They probably would not notice if someone were loading instruments and sound system equipment. The neighbor would conclude that they were preparing for a service at another location and would not give it a second thought.

Thirdly, religious facilities may be chosen for burglary because of the quick return on his efforts. Cash is the all-time favorite, followed closely by sound equipment and musical instruments. These items are easily pawned. In a household burglary, the favorite items are jewelry and cash, followed by guns, televisions, video recorders, and computers. Obviously other items are stolen, but unless a criminal finds a home with expensive jewelry he is likely to benefit more from a "church" burglary.

Additionally, it is important to remember that churches, mosques, synagogues, and temples are easily accessible. A burglar can often walk right in, look around and leave. Generally, there are no cameras, alarms, or methods of apprehension. With a little creativity and observation skills, they are usually "home free" within a matter of minutes. Also, it is important to note that many religious facilities do not lock their doors allowing easy access for the criminal. Also, religious facilities are less likely to have a barking dog.

The Congregation's Viewpoint

"We felt we had been invaded. There was a sense of rage. Our church had been violated by intruders. It raised the ire of the entire congregation," said members of the Calvary Baptist Church of Aberdeen, New Jersey, as they expressed their feelings. The burglar entered the church by forcing a door open. The item of choice was the sound equipment. The church, thinking the burglar was finished, worked diligently to replace the equipment. The burglar allowed the church sufficient time to do this and he returned, only to steal the new equipment. This is not unusual.

Crime Research

Research conducted at the University of Louisville in Louisville, Kentucky, by co-author Ratliff for her master's thesis, indicated that religious facilities are often victimized more than one time. In 1993, there were 45 reported cases of burglary in Jefferson County. Of these 45, six facilities were victimized more than once for a total of 12 incidents. In these incidents, the time span between occurrences ranged from 12 hours to 11 months with a median of three-and-a-half days and a mean of 59 days. Four (67 percent) of the six incidents occurred within one week on the initial incident and the remaining incidents occurred after four months and 11 months.

In the city of Louisville, there were 72 church burglaries and one synagogue burglary in 1993. Of this 73, eleven facilities were victimized more than once for a total of 26 incidents. Ten facilities were burglarized twice each and one facility was burglarized six times. The time span between occurrences ranged from four to 360 days with a median of 90 days and a mean of 114 days. Two of the incidents occurred within one week of the initial incident and the remaining incidents occurred between 14 days and 12 months.

Who Did It?

In addition to the problems your church will experience after a burglary, there are other questions that will puzzle you. For example, if the building is usually locked when you are not having services, who left the door open? What if there are no signs of forced-entry? Who has access to the building? Was this negligence or was it planned? Are we dealing with neighborhood kids? Was this crime committed by someone who will return to victimize our facility again? Is this the start of a series of crimes? Did the burglar take a list of church members and their addresses? There are many questions about who would commit such a crime. We cannot give you a profile of a "church burglar," but we can tell you that he or she can range in age from the very young to the elderly.

Deterring Burglars

What can you do to inhibit, deter, avoid, or prevent unlawful intrusions? First, we suggest that you request an interview and "security assessment" by a crime prevention officer from your local law enforcement agency. The crime prevention officer will review your site for security weaknesses and make recommendations for improvement. We also encourage you to schedule a meeting with the officers who patrol the area in which your facility is located. Listen carefully and take their advice, if at all possible.

It is important that the exterior of the building not serve as an "invitation" for crime. Exterior lighting is key to preventing burglary at night. Motion detectors and sensor lights deter criminals because their every move is noted. Also, it is important for the parking lot to be well lighted; thereby eliminating places for predators to hide.

Ensure that your entranceways are well lighted and that the doors are visible from the street. Practice CPTED provisions by ensuring that the bushes are trimmed away from the building and that your shrubbery and trees are properly groomed so that individuals cannot hide there before attempting a break-in. On mature trees, try to apply the "10 Foot Rule." Just make sure that all branches are trimmed to no less than eight, but preferably, ten feet. This ensures that worshipers and the police personnel driving by can easily see anyone on your grounds.

 It is important to keep all windows and doors clear so they are easily viewed from the road. You can also establish a natural boundary with plants and hedges. Thick holly or thorn bushes can be used for both barriers and aesthetic beauty. These plants are quite useful in preventing or restricting access. You can prune these plants to control the height, width, and density of the hedge. You can ensure visibility over the ornamentation if this is desirable, or you can restrict visibility if it isn't. Fences, walls, and hedges can restrict access to the individuals who you do not want to enter and they can increase the likelihood that they will enter where you prefer. While these structures can help, they can also limit the ability of large numbers of people to leave quickly. Solid wall fencing is not recommended because it restricts your ability to see the grounds and the building doorways.

Additionally, we encourage the installation of burglary/fire alarms. We say burglary/fire alarms because the most expensive aspect of a "supervised" telephone-call-out alarm is the monthly fee. It doesn't cost any more to monitor for fire than it does for both. You just incur the purchase price for the additional heat or smoke sensors.

One of the most important precautions that you can take is to compile an inventory listing of all equipment and moveable assets, marking or engraving each piece of property with identifying numbers. The inventory list should include the description of the property, the serial number, make, model, color, and purchase price. If you have an assigned Employer Identification Number (EIN), we encourage you to engrave this number on each piece of property that you have listed on your inventory list. If you do not have an EIN, you may choose any series of numbers. We encourage you to include photographs of the sound equipment, musical instruments, chalices, and silver, and copies of original invoices when the equipment was purchased. More than likely, the burglar will dispose of the stolen property (musical instruments, sound equipment, or computers) in pawnshops. The inventory listing will be helpful to the police officers attempting to trace and locate your stolen property.

We encourage facilities to establish the policy that you will not keep cash on-site and that you make deposits on the day the money is collected. We suggest that you post signs in the event a burglar is checking out your premises. Signs can be made at your local print shop or on your computer to read, DEPOSITS ARE NOT KEPT OVERNIGHT or DEPOSITS ARE MADE IMMEDIATELY FOLLOWING THE SERVICE AND ARE NOT KEPT ON-SITE. While you may need to keep a small amount of cash for petty cash, this would not be reviewed as dishonest because you have stated, "Deposits." If we are talking petty cash, petty cash is not a deposit. This simple posting could eliminate a lot of motivation because burglars would know that it is not worthwhile to pursue a break-in. We also encourage you to post signs on the safe and in the office that states, RECORDS ONLY–NO CASH. Small, but expensive items should be stored in a safe. The safe should be secured to the floor with heavy bolts that prevent the burglars from removing it. However, the safe should be clearly marked with a permanent sign that reads WE DO NOT KEEP MONEY IN THIS SAFE.

Additionally, it is important to keep your checks and credit cards under lock and key, preferably locked in a safe. Always know the amount of the last check you wrote and have it listed in a separate location. Burglars often steal the last check or two, so the church treasurer doesn't know that any checks are missing until he or she gets to that page or receives a forged canceled check. A good treasurer will have a separate list of credit card numbers and the phone numbers to cancel the cards in the event they are stolen, as well as a list of checking account numbers and the bank's phone number. As a reminder, you should never have blank checks with a signature already on them because this really makes it easy for the criminal to go shopping.

If you have ministries requiring monetary resources, consider using checks only or vouchers. Criminals may approach you for financial assistance during business hours for the purpose of determining where you keep your cash. For example, they may approach you and request a relatively small amount, but once they discover where you keep the cash they return later for the full amount. By using checks or vouchers, their incentive to steal is limited.

In addition to access control from the parking lot and entry doors, we encourage locking procedures, key control, and inventory. We also encourage you to keep your facility locked at all times. If having a Sunday morning service, only allow access through the front doors and ensure that they are locked after the service is over. It is also important to make sure no one entered the building and is hiding or that anyone tampered with other doors, windows, or locks. Also, it is strongly recommended that you have a formalized locking procedure that includes a walk through after each service by your security team of guards or volunteers.

Key control means that you maintain a list of everyone who has keys to your building(s). If someone moves or begins worship elsewhere, you need to collect their keys. Additionally, if you change pastors, priests, or rabbis you should get your locks re-keyed, issuing keys as needed. It is imperative to know who has the keys, so keep an up-to-date record on everyone who has a key to the building. This will help in the event of a burglary and there are no signs of a forced entry. Until an arrest has been made, everyone in the congregation is a suspect. Individuals with keys would be considered prime suspects. You need to be prepared to give law enforcement officers a list of those who have keys in their possession.

Spare keys should be under lock and key in a locked cabinet, or in a separate locked closet. The keys should be mounted on a board so that the person responsible for the keys will immediately know if one is missing. If you want key security, stay away from master keys. One master key lost or stolen means you have to re-key everything. The average church member will not need an exterior door key because the doors will be opened at the appropriate hours.

Additionally, you should implement a policy that does not allow members to work alone in the buildings. It is recommended that you encourage group work or that individuals work at the times others are present on-site. For example, someone can work in one area of the church while a class is conducted or someone can work in a classroom while the youths are in the gym. We suggest that you schedule multiple events at the same time.

We also encourage all facilities to install a phone. It is important to be able to call the police in the event of an emergency. Also, if an alarm is going off, the alarm company and police department need to be notified.

Door and window locks need to be secure. This includes more than the common single latch in the middle of the window. Reinforcement locks should be installed at the top of the windows. Stained glass windows need sufficient reinforcement or a sensor detector attached to the glass. Several of the facilities we studied installed metal mesh on the stained glass windows. Others installed clear Plexiglas on the outside to prevent accidental breakage and vandalism.

Back doors and doors that are not visible from the street should be top priority when making a security assessment. Prior to making these changes, we encourage you to check with your local fire marshal for compliance with fire codes. Doors are very important because most burglars gain entrance through a doorway. In residential burglaries, almost 90 percent of all burglars enter through a doorway.

Only about 10 percent go through windows, skylights, or air-conditioning vents. We don't know the percentage of church entranceway burglaries, but the crime prevention value of a strong doorframe system is incalculable. The doorframe system includes reinforced door openings, solid wood or metal doors, and quality locks. All exterior door locks should be reinforced with metal guard plates or rings designed to prevent the unlawful removal of key cylinders. Often astragals (exterior metal plates) are also installed with rounded bolts from the outside to prevent access or manipulation of lock-bolts.

Exterior doors that swing out must be fitted with non-removable hinge pins or the standard pins may be welded into place. Preferably, all hinges should be located on the inside and the exterior doors should swing in. On retrofits, alter this access with the non-removable hinge pins or a weld.

Automatic photoelectric switches on the exterior lights above doors and non-accessible windows are also advantageous and worth the investment. Pay particular attention to fire exits. Most fire exit doors are steel plated and are difficult to enter from the outside. However, since most of these doors have what are called panic bars, a gum wrapper in the door-lock receptacle can compromise them from within. The door "looks" locked from the inside, but in reality it has been compromised. The door itself must be pushed, not the bar, to see if it is actually secure.

Windows are the second most likely point of entry. Whoever locks your facility after any service should check all windows, particularly ground floor windows, or windows casually accessible from adjacent buildings to ensure that they are locked. Windows which can be casually accessed and are large enough to permit entrance, should have an inside key lock. Sometimes windows are open during certain seasons of the year. A window "block" will prevent the window being opened more than eight or nine inches, allowing ventilation, but inhibiting intrusion.

Protecting Office Equipment

There are many new security companies selling protective devices. Computer, copier, and fax lock-downs are just a few equipment-lock examples. These security devices are made of chains, security cables, locking hardware, and locking bolts. They "lock" expensive office equipment to desks and tables. Your sound equipment should be treated similarly. Sometimes chains, security cable, and other forms of locking hardware are used. The function of the equipment is to slow down a thief. If the thief has to make noise, use a hacksaw, or tear up a desk to steal a computer, chances are he or she will go somewhere else.

Important business records and personnel files should be kept in a locked fire-resistant metal file cabinet. While these cabinets can easily be broken into, they aren't often the targets of church burglars, especially if they are marked "Business Records" on the door of the unit.

Church "Watch" Programs

Are there any programs to help churches, mosques, synagogues, or temples prevent crime? Yes. A "Church Watch" program was initiated in Tacoma, Washington, after a series of religious facility burglaries. Operated similarly to a "Neighborhood Watch" or "Block Watch" program, the "Church Watch" program was designed to encourage neighbors around church sites, whether members or non-members, to observe the activities on church grounds and to note any unusual events. This program has been quite successful in many areas, so we encourage you to work with the neighbors in your area and to give them names and numbers to call in the event they see anything unusual.

Your Overall Crime Deterrence Approach

One security improvement alone will not lower your risk substantially. If you implement a program, however, you can lower the likelihood that your facility will be burgled. The rules are simple and are the same rules that apply at your home, office, or workplace. If the rule is good at home, in the neighborhood, or at the workplace, it is probably a good rule for your house of worship as well.

Endnotes

1. *Chicago* (IL) *Chicago Tribune* article of 15 September, 1994, n.p.

2. K. Crowley and E. Browne, "Organist Preyed on 500 Churches," *New York Post*, 4 January 1992, (Newsbank 1992 LAW 1:D12), n.p.

CHAPTER 6

VANDALISM

The First Baptist Church of Crete, Illinois, was vandalized three times in one month. The first incident occurred at the church annex, less than a mile from the main church. The annex building and a white church van in the parking lot were spray-painted with "satanic-type wording." Less than three weeks later, church members arrived to find a decapitated black cat left outside the church's main entrance. Blood was found on the central air-conditioning unit outside the church as an indication that the cat was killed on-site. Several weeks later, the pastor discovered a dead raccoon hanging on the main doorway one Sunday morning. After the third occasion, a representative of the Will County Sheriff's Office said they were keeping an eye on a local teen whom they described as a devil worshiper.[1]

In Los Angeles, California, four Catholic churches were vandalized in an AIDS protest. Vandals, referring to themselves as activists, splattered bright red paint on the churches to protest Los Angeles Archbishop Roger M. Mahony's condemnation of the use of condoms to fight the spread of AIDS. A spokesman for the activists, who was part of a newly formed group called Greater Religious Responsibilities! (GRR) said the members of the group also pasted posters featuring a full face photo of Archbishop Mahony that read, "Safe sex is a lie and a fraud," and "Murderer." According to the spokesman, about 20 people were involved in the project.[2]

In Denver, Colorado, vandals defaced at least 300 headstones and left inflammatory messages painted on the outside of a local Catholic church. The tombstones were covered in plastic bags with red or orange painted "AIDS" messages on them. Signs found at the cemetery carried messages, "Jesus Died of AIDS," and "Blessed Virgin Mary Sez: No latex. No Sex," and "Pope–Join the Boycott," referring to the boycott of Colorado since voters passed Amendment 2, which prohibits any laws protecting the rights of gays.

"It's a message of anger toward the church, perhaps toward the pope. It's a demonstration of hostility and contempt against the church, meant to disrupt and terrorize many of those who have loved ones buried at the cemetery," said Tim McCutcheon, director of finances for the diocese. In a similar vandalism incident at the Basilica of the Immaculate Conception in Denver, a statue of the Virgin Mary was splattered with red paint and covered with a plastic bag depicting a condom.[3] This criminal act was in response to the church's stand against homosexuality and it cost the church and its insurers thousands of dollars in repairs, not to mention the trauma family members experienced when the tombstones of loved ones were defaced.

Again, in Denver, Colorado, vandals also splattered red paint and scrawled angry graffiti messages at the Cathedral of Immaculate Conception. Parishioners arriving for early mass discovered the steps of the cathedral smeared with red paint. According to an unidentified caller to the local television channel, the vandalism was the work of a group calling themselves Citizens Concerned About Aids, in an apparent effort to draw more attention to the plight of Americans infected by the AIDS virus. The vandalism came one day after Archbishop J. Francis Stafford announced a multimillion dollar renovation of the cathedral in anticipation of Pope John Paul II's planned visit to Denver in August 1993.[4]

In Everet, Massachusetts, a Jewish cemetery and a synagogue were vandalized as the nation memorialized the Nazi Holocaust. On the evening of President Bill Clinton's dedication of the United States Holocaust Memorial Museum in Washington D.C., more than 100 tombstones were toppled and many were spray-painted with swastikas. A building in the cemetery was spray-painted with a birthday salute to Adolf Hitler. The synagogue's front wall was defaced with nine swastikas and the phrase, "Jew Boy, Remember." The writings also included the word "Skins," an apparent reference to neo-Nazi skinheads. The German word for Jew, "Judge" was scrawled nearby.

"This is not a prank," said Rabbi Abraham Morhaim. "Young kids don't know the German word for Jew. This is an ugly reminder that anti-Semitism is alive even in this late stage of the 20th century." This event underscored what political and religious leaders described as growing concern over the rise of neo-Nazism in Europe and increasing anti-Semitic violence in the United States.[5] Three males were arrested and charged with "hundreds of accounts" of malicious destruction of property, as well as desecrating a holy place and civil rights violations, after they returned from Washington D.C., where they had protested the dedication of the United States Holocaust Memorial Museum.[6]

Teenagers Are Often Accused

Knowing that most vandalism occurs during the summer months and on weekends, we normally associate vandalism with bored teenagers. However, vandalism has evolved into a crime associated with social prejudice, religious prejudice, racial supremacy, gangs, radical gay rights activism, the woman's right to choose movement, the pro-life movement, and satanic ritualism. It involves much more than just graffiti and has resulted in extensive (and expensive) damages to houses of worship, businesses, and public facilities. Much of the religious vandalism expressed sends a specific public policy message to the victimized congregation.

Vandalism Reflects Social Prejudice

In our research on crimes in churches, mosques, synagogues, and temples, we discovered many prejudices associated with cases of vandalism. For example, Jewish synagogues are most often vandalized with hate symbols. In 1999, the total number of anti-Semitic incidents reported to the Anti-Defamation League, including acts against both property and persons was 1,547. This total comprised reports from 39 states

> **Vandalism is frequently defined as "an act of destruction in which monetary profit is not a prime motive.** Criminologists and crime prevention specialists have found that many, if not most, acts of vandalism are not premeditated but are spontaneous outbursts of rage at an attractive, available, target. However, vandalism committed at religious institutions seems to be directly based on prejudice, hatred, and fear.

and the District of Columbia.[7] The five states reporting the highest totals of anti-Semitic incidents of all kinds during 1999 were New York (352), California (275), New Jersey (226), Massachusetts (111), and Florida (88).[8] *The 1999 Audit of Anti-Semitic Incidents* report indicates that vandalism of Jewish institutions declined by four percent during the last year,[9] however it is still a significant number.

Some houses of worship have been vandalized in response to the notoriety of a single church member. When John Demjanjuk was convicted of Nazi war crimes in Israel in April 1988, vandals spray painted the Catholic church he attended here in the United States.[10] It is interesting that the perpetrators of this offense connected the criminal to the church and chose to take action against the church rather than against the individual.

Houses of worship are often targeted for vandalism because of their conservative stand on politicized issues such as abortion, gay rights, and premarital sex. Individuals who strongly disagree with specific doctrines and teachings have decided to become "anti-religion adversaries." While the vandals (who refer to themselves as activists) are attempting to draw public attention to the issues, they are ignoring the doctrinal teachings and are trying to influence religious and public policies. It is interesting that individuals would rather "act out" and desecrate a house of worship rather than leave to find a worship center that more closely practices his or her personal belief system.

Worship centers are also vandalized by Satan worshipers. Dead animals have been left on the church steps.[11] Blood, sometimes human blood, has been sprinkled in and outside the church. Buildings, buses, and vans have been painted with satanic symbols. It appears that some cults encourage vandalizing a place of worship as part of the initiation requirements. The specific messages painted in the graffiti gives the vandal a sense of power. The sacrilege of the event increases his or her satisfaction, especially if Satan worship is also involved.

Additionally, individuals marking their "gang territory" vandalize houses of worship. This is done by painting their name and gang symbols on the exterior of the building, the doors, or the sign. While these symbols don't identify the building as gang property, the symbols signify boundaries over which the gang claims control. Rival gangs know that they are to stay out of this territory—or they will end up in a fight.

Graffiti and Other Forms of Vandalism

Windows and doors have been broken. Vehicles have been scratched, dented, and spray-painted. Walls have been painted with graffiti symbolisms and pews, furnishings, artwork, and musical instruments have been damaged.

The most popular form of vandalism is graffiti written on exterior or interior walls. Vandals either damage the exterior of the building or spray paint the interior. The interior is more attractive because once they have entered the facility they are out of sight of police or neighbors. Additionally, our research has discovered many cases in which windows and glass doors are broken, often by bottles, bricks, or bullets. Glass breakage, especially if it is of expensive stained glass, is a frequent desecration, as is the assault on ornamental architecture or the cemetery grounds.

It is important to note that vandalism often conceals another crime. For example, vandalism on the interior often occurs after someone has broken in, intending to commit a burglary, but is unsuccessful because of quality locks or safes. They displace their aggression by vandalizing the facility, by turning over desks, file cabinets, and office equipment. On the other hand, there may not be anything that the burglar wants to steal, so he seeks revenge and leaves his mark through vandalism. If the burglar does not fear arrest, he or she may resort to staying inside for a longer period of time and committing other crimes. The longer the criminal stays on-site, the more the likelihood that you will experience vandalism or other extraneous damage. Most burglars, however, only use force at their points of entry and exit, making little noise, and leaving as quickly as possible.

However, when a burglar resorts to vandalism by "trashing" the area, this makes it difficult for the church administrator and the law enforcement officers to determine what has been stolen versus what has been misplaced. This is why we encourage administrators to lock offices, desks, file cabinets, and safes. Likewise, interior office doors should be locked and doors separating the offices from the sanctuary or other areas should be locked. This delays the criminals travel through your buildings. We realize that locks may be picked or forced open. However, it will take longer and may discourage the opportunist from continuing. Dr. Gennaro Vito, professor at the University of Louisville, National Crime Prevention Institute, and the Southern Police Institute, encourages lock usage. "Even criminals should have to work for a living," he says.

In some vandalism cases, the individual has entered the building with the intent to set a fire; however, he may change his mind when he cannot find chemicals to assist him, or he is impeded by fire-retardant carpets or drapes. Depending on his frustration level and the fear of apprehension, he or she, may then resort to vandalism.

How Can You Avoid Vandalism?

Vandalism, like many other crimes, can be deterred. It is *your* responsibility to take precautions to reduce the potential for this crime to occur. There are many ways to reduce the potential for victimization. Good security against street crime, parking lot crime, robbery, rape, and burglary is also good security for the vandalism problem. The basics include locking doors and having well-lighted doors, windows, and parking lots. Extras include limiting access to the parking lot after services and at night. We often encourage the purchase of security cameras. Some facilities purchase intrusion detection devices, smoke detectors, and fire alarms as general crime prevention strategies against vandalism.

Your crime prevention plan should include a section for exterior and interior precautions. First, it is important to secure the exterior. You should review the lighting in the parking lot and around the building, in addition to reviewing the parking lot and eliminating casual access to the property by reducing the number of entrances and exits. Second, it is recommended that you block the drive around and behind your building to deter individuals from parking behind the building. If left open, you may be providing "cover" for criminal activity. It is not uncommon for other crimes to occur behind the building such as drug use and sale and sexual activity.

Vandalism occurs mostly at night, so if the parking lot is secured then the potential for victimization is reduced. If individuals cannot drive onto your parking lot, then they are forced to walk. If walking, they face the potential for having to run if their presence is noticed. If the exterior of the building is well lighted, then the vandal can't hide in darkness while defacing the exterior of the building or "keying" vehicles parked on the premises. We encourage the use of motion activated lights and dusk-to-dawn lights throughout your property.

Some congregations install polycarbonate sheets over expensive stained and curved glass windows. Often these sheets are applied both inside and outside the window. These sheets weigh 50 percent to 60 percent less than glass and have over 250 times the impact strength of regular glass.[12] They have thirty times the strength of the less expensive acrylic panels. These panels are less weather resistant than glass but normally can be serviceable for seven to 10 years in outside installations. In some applications, such as beachfront properties or desert use, these panels may be scratched sooner and require more rapid replacement.

Exterior Precautions

- Have a *definable perimeter*. This can be accomplished with walls, fences, or hedges.
- Have good exterior lighting.
- Design the building so that most of it is visible from the street.
- Limit access to the "back side" of the building.
- Limit access to the parking lot after church hours.
- Ask your local law enforcement agency to drive through the parking lot when activities are not in session.
- Participate in a "church-block watch" with your neighbors.
- Use "anti-climb" paint on guttering material and rain drains to prevent individuals from climbing to windows or roofs. This should be at least 8 ft. high. This paint doesn't dry, ever, and is very slippery.
- Protect your windows with unbreakable glazing or polycarbonate sheets placed over your expensive stained glass windows.

When thinking about crime prevention, one must remember that houses of worship are more vulnerable to many crimes because of irregular architecture and a multiplicity of entrances and exits. The architectural design may not include many windows for outside surveillance. The doors may be large and easily pried open. New churches, synagogues, and mosques are typically built in secluded locations because worshipers need large parking areas, while many of the older pre-existing structures remain in the inner city. Both the remote location and the inner-city location pose unique security risks. These buildings may not be easily surveilled from the road; thereby restricting law enforcement scrutiny while on routine patrol. Once inside the buildings, the many hallways, meeting rooms, cabinets, and closets provide hiding spaces for all that hold ill will against religious institutions.

If your facility has buses and/or vans, ensure that they are parked in a well-lighted area and that they are parked far enough apart so that trespassers can be spotted. Vandals intending to "do a little painting" will feel very uncomfortable in lighted areas, and will not feel as free to exercise their artwork.

As mentioned in previous chapters we further recommend that the church be "searched" prior to locking up after services. If certain areas are not used during the service, they should be locked at that time.

Another method of limiting vandalism is to build your rectory, parsonage, manse, vicarage, or pastorium on the properties adjacent to the church. If your parsonage is in a house across town, you may choose to move a modular home to your properties. Let a staff member live there. This method is applied successfully in many rural school districts. You, too, will lower your vandalism problem, especially in rural or remote areas.

Limit Access to Groundskeeper Tools

Remember that your tools can be used in the commission of "your" crime. Be very careful to control access to groundskeeper's tools. Ladders left outside increase the likelihood of both burglary and vandalism. If you need a ladder at your building, store it inside a locked room, or build a secure outbuilding for storage with a good lock. If a ladder is strapped to the exterior of the outbuilding, protect the ladder and your property with a padlocked metal strap or a lock chain running from inside the building. Some ladders are padlocked from bolts drilled through inside outbuilding walls. Whatever limits access or restricts access is the key to lowering your vulnerability.

Be on Your Guard

You need to be watchful and take precautions to protect your properties. If you believe that crime will never happen in your community, your child's school, or your church, you increase the likelihood of the crime's occurrence by your ignorance. By doing nothing, you are increasing the likelihood that crimes will occur. We all must take responsibility and do our part to protect ourselves, our property, and to ensure that our houses of worship are protected. The responsibility for crime prevention lies with each member of the congregation.

Interior Precautions

- Secure the interior of the building.
- Lock all exterior doors and windows.
- Keep doors, storage closets, and cabinets locked.
- Maintain key security.
- Do not store items (like paint) which may be used to vandalize.
- Install an alarm system.
- Install motion detection lights on your exterior doorways and near your parking lots.

Endnotes

1. T. Tierney, "Vandal Eludes Cops: Upsets Crete Pastor," *Chicago Tribune*, 12 December, 1994, p. C7.

2. Ronald L. Soble, "Four Catholic Churches Defaced in AIDS Protest," *Los Angeles Times*, 4 December, 1989, n.p.

3. Tracy Seipel and Virginia Culver, "Vandals Strike at Catholic Cemetery: AIDS Messages Are Left, Markers, Statues Damaged," *Denver (Colo.) Post*, 15 January, 1993, n.p.

4. Joseph B. Verrengia, "AIDS Activists Vandalize Capitol, Cathedral," *Denver* (Colo.) *Rocky Mountain News*, 2 December, 1992, n.p.

5. Bob Hohler, "Synagogue, Jewish Graves Desecrated: Swastikas Are Painted in Everett Cemetery, on Peabody Temple," *Boston Globe*, 22 April, 1993, n.p.

6. J. Heney, "Vandal Suspects Linked to neo-Nazis," *Boston Herald*, 24 April, 1993, n.p.

7. Anti-Defamation League, *Audit of Anti-Semitic Incidents 1999* (New York: Anti-Defamation League, 2000), p. 3.

8. Anti-Defamation League, *Audit of Anti-Semitic Incidents 1999* (New York: Anti-Defamation League, 2000), p. 9.

9. Anti-Defamation League, *Audit of Anti-Semitic Incidents 1999* (New York: Anti-Defamation League, 2000), p. 8.

10. Michael Newton and Judy Ann Newton, *Racial and Religious Violence in America: A Chronology*. (New York: Garland Publishing, 1991), p. 648.

11. T. Tierney, "Vandal Eludes Cops: Upsets Crete Pastor, " *Chicago Tribune*, 12 December, 1994, n.p.

12. C. H. Kelly. *Church Security*, [Staffordshire, England Police] (New Castle, United Kingdom: Priory Publications, May 1989), n.p.

CHAPTER 7

CHURCH ARSON

Early one Sunday morning, Dr. Charles Quarles[1], pastor of the Hickory Ridge Baptist Church in Memphis, Tennessee, opened his church office door to the strong smell of smoke. Fortunately, the fire was minor. Looking down the hall, he saw a charred line burned in the carpet and that the building had been vandalized. After calling the police, he surveyed the damage and discovered that the burglar/arsonist had forced open a window to accomplish the crime. The damage was minimal and the church members were grateful for the fire resistant and retardant carpets and draperies. Another church, a short distance away, was burned to the ground that same night.

Our research depicts many examples of arson. Big, small, rural, urban, Protestant, Catholic, synagogues, temples, and mosques have all been victimized. The threat of fire is perhaps the single greatest danger your house of worship faces today.[2] While many fires are accidental, caused by frayed wiring or by leaving kitchen equipment on, the National Safety Council says arson fires strike seven churches every day in the U.S. and that the toll is continually increasing.[3] Arson is the leading cause of fires at worship centers.[4]

Co-author Ratliff has researched church arsons for many years. Church arsons were frequent in the 1950s and the 1960s. In June 1993, David Snyder, staff writer for the New Orleans (Louisiana) *Times Picayune* reported that in the 1960s some 34 churches with black congregations in Mississippi were apparently torched. One of the most comprehensive articles was published in the *New York City Post* in 1992 and titled, "Trial By Fire," in which the author reported worship center fires in Florida, Arizona, and Tennessee.[5] Listed below is a summary of the article:

1. January 1991, in Gainesville, Florida, a landmark church built in 1907 was destroyed when an arsonist set fire at the altar.

2. February 1991, in Fort Myers, Sanford, and Orange County, Florida, an arsonist set fires to 28 churches during February 1991. The attacks were ecumenical, impacting many denominations.

3. March 1991, in Merritt Island, Florida, someone smashed a stained-glass window and set fire to a chapel.

4. August and September 1991, in East Ridge, Tennessee, an arsonist set fire to five churches.

5. September 1991, in Phoenix, Arizona, an arsonist destroyed a $4.25 million worship facility.

6. October 1991, in Lake City, Gainsville, and Ocala, Florida, an arsonist set fire to seven churches.

7. October and November 1991, in Winter Haven, Daytona Beach, St. Augustine, Jacksonville Beach, and Gainsville, Florida, an arsonist set fire to eight churches within a three-week period.

One arsonist seemed to be responsible for these attacks against houses of worship. The burnings stopped on November 8 after police focused their investigation on a drifter, who was arrested on November 12.

Research shows that there have always been church arsons. In December 1987, in Cambridge, Massachusetts, a church nativity scene was burned by arsonists, who left behind a dead sparrow, a severed cow's tongue, and a note reading: "How many more fires before you realize God is dead?" Authorities believed voodoo cultists were linked to a series of church fires in eastern Massachusetts.[6]

In McComb, Mississippi, two predominantly African-American churches were burned to the ground in apparent acts of arson, bringing back painful images of the violent 1960s.[7] In June of 1993, a fire set by an arsonist destroyed a church in West Palm Beach, Florida.[8]

Bombings

On January 16, 1988, in Kamas, Utah, a bomb blast caused $1 million dollars damage to a local Mormon chapel. Authorities surrounded a polygamist compound at nearby Marion, seeking suspects in the case, but the cult held off police with gunfire for 12 days. The siege ended in a shootout that left one police officer dead and a cult leader wounded.[9]

On Sunday, May 24, 1998, an explosion at a church in Danville, Illinois, injured 33 members of the congregation, several of them seriously. Members reported smelling gunpowder after the explosion. This was quite a charge. The force of the explosion shattered windows 100 yards away while glass and twisted metal littered the street.[10]

Special Agent Jerry Singer with the Bureau of Alcohol, Tobacco and Firearms said that a similar incident occurred December 30, 1987, in Oakwood, Illinois, about fifteen miles from the Danville church. He reported that the blast killed one church volunteer.[11] These bombings received very little media coverage.

The Religious Institution Arson Problem

National statistics on church arson are not available because crimes that occur on religious properties are not separately or distinctly reported to the Justice Department in a religious institution format. However, our research indicates that church arson was occurring throughout the country for many years prior to the increased scrutiny in 1996. One primary indication of church arson comes from insurance companies. In 1987, the Church Mutual Insurance Company processed 2,531 church claims that resulted in payments of over $15.4 million: $8.4 million was for arson damage and $1 million for burglary losses.

In January 1995, the Bureau of Alcohol, Tobacco, and Firearms began to track church arson. By June 1996, they reported that since January 1995, 48 church arsons had occurred. Twenty-five of the purposeful fires were at predominantly African-American churches and 23 were at predominantly white churches. Yet, this is not what we heard from the media.

Church arson is often described as a racial issue and a hate crime. During 1996, the media focused much of their attention on the issue of church arson, claiming racial hatred as the motive. The media discussed it in terms of "black and white" churches, and how racism was prevalent. The focus on this topic prompted Congress to establish a fund for churches that were burned and the Church Arson Prevention Act was passed.

Church arson was often quoted as being one of America's most alarming crime trends during the summer of 1996. While white churches were also burned, there seemed to be a disproportionate percentage of "torched" African-American facilities. In response, the Federal government established a National Church Arson Task Force, comprised of arson investigators from the Treasury and Justice Departments and criminologists from throughout the country, to examine the church arson problem. This funding also created a special team of lawyer/prosecutors to rapidly respond to suspected church arsons, working with local investigators and the Federal task force agents. Other agents worked with local churches on prevention approaches.

Beginning in 1996, but picking up a caseload of church fires dating back to 1995, the National Church Arson Task Force set precedent-making history. They opened 670 active cases on arsons, bombings, or attempted bombings occurring between January 1, 1995, and September 8, 1998. Federal, state, and local law enforcement officials arrested 308 suspects in connection with 230 of these cases. This resulted in a 34 percent arrest rate, nearly double the 16 percent arrest rate nationwide.

Two-hundred-and-thirty-five defendants have already been convicted in connection with 173 arson or bombings of houses of worship during this time period.[12]

The Federal Response

The Department of Justice has awarded over $3 million to counties in 13 states to intensify their law enforcement and surveillance efforts regarding vulnerable houses of worship, and the Federal Emergency Management Agency (FEMA) awarded more than $1.5 million to state and local governments to enhance the quality of arson investigation and prevention training services. FEMA has partnered with over 300 organizations to prevent arson and it coordinates the National Arson Prevention Clearinghouse and its $1.5 million technical assistance requests, as well as providing training for investigation and prevention.

The Federal government has reaffirmed its commitment to expending the time, resources, and effort necessary to solve church arsons and to prosecute those who are responsible by creating a more permanent institutional approach to the handling of these cases. During the fall of 1999, the task force lodged responsibility for federal prosecution in the Criminal Section of the Civil Rights Division, the existing structure within the Justice Department that has jurisdiction over church arson and other federal criminal civil rights cases.[13]

The Federal Church Arson Prevention Grant Program

In 1996, Congress set aside $6 million dollars for the Church Arson Prevention Grant Program. Each county in states where burnings occurred was eligible for a one-time award grant to enhance security measures including increased police patrols, investigation expenses, and education efforts aimed at ending church arson.

In Jefferson County, Kentucky, the county arson bureau received a grant to provide technical assistance to worship centers. Crime prevention specialists visited nearly every facility in Jefferson County conducting security and fire assessments. After preparing the reports, they mailed them to each facility. Interestingly enough, it was noted that not one single church responded to their report by calling with questions or to say "thanks."[14]

Additionally, the Church Arson Prevention Act was amended to make it a federal violation if religious property is damaged because of its racial or ethnic character. Prior to the amendment, federal violations applied only to cases of damage based on the religious character of the property. The bill also authorized victims of church burnings to receive compensation from the crime victims' trust funds.

Additionally, task forces were appointed on the federal, state, and local levels to ensure a swift response. A major goal of the Federal Task Force was to prepare a church arson report to the president of the United States. In January 1997, the National Church Arson Task Force submitted an interim report to the president.

It concluded that during the period of January 1, 1995, to January 7, 1997, there were 328 arson/bombing investigations nationwide. Of those, 190 (58 percent) were in other houses of worship and 138 (42 percent) were in African-American houses of worship. Additionally, during that time frame, 143 (33 percent) arrests were made in relationship to these cases. The remaining 221 (68 percent) cases were still pending. These involved the arrests of 143 individuals.[15]

There were 34 arsons and three bombings at African-American houses of worships in which arrests were made. Of the individuals arrested, 66.7 percent were Caucasian subjects and 31.5 percent were African-American subjects. Of the non-African-American houses of worship in which an arrest was made, there were 67 arsons and three bombings. The percentage of Caucasians arrested was 89.4 while 8.2 percent arrested were African-American.

> ### The National Church Arson Task Force Interim Report Found
> ### (January 1, 1995, to January 7, 1977)
>
> - There were 328 arson/bombing cases in 1995 and 1996.
> - A total of 42 percent of these were at African American churches.
> - Fifty-seven percent of these were at "other" churches.
> - Arrests were made in 34 arsons and 3 bombings at African-American churches.
> - Arrests were made in 67 arsons and 3 bombings in "other" churches.
> - Fifty-four suspects were arrested for African-American church arsons; 36 were white, 17 were African-American, and one was Hispanic.
> - Eighty-five suspects were arrested for arson in non-African-American churches; 76 were white, seven were African-American, and two were Hispanic.
> - Forty-eight defendants were convicted in connection with 43 worship center arsons.

During 1996, arson cases at 16 African-American houses of worship and 171 "other" houses of worship were cleared.

The report was not given much coverage by the media, as it was no longer a hot news topic when it was released in January 1997. While 328 investigations during a two-year period are significant, the average number of arsons each year is only 164. Divided amongst the 50 states, the average number of arsons committed is

3.2 per state each year. We know that the fires were concentrated in the South and, particularly, in the rural South where the availability of fire trucks and water hydrants are reduced. Research indicates that there is more arson in the South than in other parts of the country.[16]

Precautions to Prevent Arson

It is important that each church take precautions to reduce the victimization risk. Individuals who have entered the building surreptitiously often set fires. Arsonists light books, curtains, altars, carpets, and other flammables once inside the building. However, if the building is secured and an intruder cannot gain entry, then the building is relatively safe. If an arsonist cannot easily enter the church, he will have to set the fire outside the building or on the roof, which increases the likelihood of the fire being quickly observed by neighbors and increases the possibility of arrest. Sometimes, burning objects or bombs are thrown through windows. By having secured and/or laminated windows, you could eliminate or significantly reduce this possibility.

Additionally, make certain that you do not have combustible and inflammable materials stored in your building. If you have stockpiled these items, remove them. Stored combustibles and inflammables give an arsonist the chemicals he needs to torch your building. If there is an accidental fire, the combustible and inflammable materials will ensure that more damage occurs.

Why Do Arsonists Set Fires?

Why would someone start a church fire? Some arsonists suffer from *pyromania*, an irresistible urge to set fires. Pyromaniacs receive sexual satisfaction from watching the fire, fanning the fire, flames, and smoke. Many perpetrators also may enjoy the excitement of emergency responses, lights, sirens, and the frenetic activity of fire response teams. Sometimes homeless individuals set fires in the winter to keep warm, while others set fires by accident as the result of smoking. Other spiritually confused arsonists have confessed to trying to fulfill scripture by "destroying the earth with fire." Some are angry with religious or denominational leaders or members of the targeted church, for one reason or another. Regardless of the reasons, most individuals who set fires are neurotic and in many cases psychopathic.

Accidental Fires

Since an accidental fire is still an incredible security risk to worshipers, you need to take every precaution that is appropriate. First, ask a fire prevention specialist to give your facility a risk assessment. Listen to your consultant carefully. Do what he or she suggests. You can also get an excellent church fire prevention guide from the U.S. Bureau of Alcohol, Tobacco, and Fire-arms, the Federal agency primarily charged with

investigating the crime and from the Church Mutual Insurance Company. It is called the "Church Threat Assessment Guide."

Secondly, do not store flammable items such as paint in any area close to your furnace or heating unit. Keep your storage areas neat and clean. Don't let residues or combustibles accumulate needlessly. Don't keep gasoline containers inside your building. Secure petroleum products in a locked outbuilding.

> Faulty wiring is the second most common cause of fires at worship centers. Many facilities are old, and in some instances may even predate the use of electricity. Consequently, the wiring in some older buildings may not be adequate to handle the electrical demands of air conditioning, P.A. systems, organs, and other appliances and equipment found in worship centers today. If your building is more than 30 years old, you should probably have the wiring inspected by a qualified electrical contractor.[17]

Lightning also causes many institutional fires every year. When the steeple of co-author Quarles' church was repainted, a lightning rod was installed as a fire prevention device. Additionally, every congregation should be careful with candles during regular services, weddings, and special seasonal services.

Fires have destroyed or damaged many religious structures. Taking the precautions we recommend, listening to the suggestions of your local fire prevention personnel, and being prepared and properly insured will reduce the trauma associated with this crime or with accidental fire. Remember that sprinklers, fire extinguishers, and smoke alarms are important equipment at every house of worship.

Endnotes

1. Son of co-author Chester L. Quarles.

2. The Church Mutual Insurance Company, "Fire Safety at Your Worship Center," (Merrill, Wis.: 1998), p. 1.

3. The Church Mutual Insurance Company. "Crime Proof Your Church," The Church Mutual Protection Series (Merrill, Wis.: The Church Mutual Insurance Company, 1998), p. 2.

4. Ibid.

5. Patty Shillington, "Trial by Fire," *New York City Post*, 14 January, 1992, n.p.

6. Michael Newton and Judy Ann Newton, *Racial and Religious Violence in America: A Chronology* (New York: Garland Publishing, Incorporated, 1991), p. 646.

7. D. Snyder, "Mississippi Burning: When Two Black Churches in Rural Mississippi Were Burned to the Ground Recently in Apparent Acts of Arson, It Brought Back Painful Images of the Violent 1960's," *New Orleans* (La.) *Times Picayune*, 3 June, 1993, n.p.

8. J. Staletovich, "Spiritual Leaders Steadfast Amid Crime, Poverty," *The Palm Beach* (Fla.) *Post,* 24 July, 1993, n.p.

9. Michael Newton and Judy Ann Newton, *Racial and Religious Violence in America: A Chronology*, (New York: Garland Publishing, Incorporated, 1991), p. 646.

10. Gannet News Service, and AP Dispatches, "Explosion at Church Injures 33," *Louisville* (Ky.) *Courier Journal*, 25 May, 1988, p. A1.

11. Ibid. '

12. National Church Arson Task Force, "Second Year Report of the National Church Arson Task Force," p. 2 of 21 [cited 20 November, 2000]. Available from the U.S. Department of Justice@www.usdoj.gov/crt/church_arson/arson98.html; INTERNET.

13. National Church Arson Task Force, "Second Year Report of the National Church Arson Task Force," p. 6 of 21 [cited 20 November, 2000]. Available from the U.S. Department of Justice@www.usdoj.gov/crt/church_arson/arson98.html; INTERNET.

14. Lead investigator. Private interview with Paula Ratliff. Louisville, KY, Spring 2001.

15. National Church Arson Task Force, "Interim Report" (January 1, 1995–January 7, 1997) (Washington, D.C.: National Church Arson Task Force, October 1998), n.p.

16. National Church Arson Task Force, "Second Year Report of the National Church Arson Task Force," p.7 of 21 [cited 20 November, 2000]. Available from the U.S. Department of Justice@www.usdoj.gov/crt/church_arson/arson98.html; INTERNET.

17. The Church Mutual Insurance Company. "Fire Safety at Your Worship Center," (Merrill, Wis.: The Church Mutual Insurance Company, 1998), p. 2.

CHAPTER 8

EMBEZZLEMENT AND CON GAMES

On June 25, 1999, the front page of the *Louisville* (Ky.) *Courier Journal* read "Church Loss to Gambling is $11,000; Pastor Held." The article stated that a 23-year-old New Albany, Indiana, pastor allegedly took $11,000 from his church accounts and gambled it away at the River Boat casino in Harrison County.

The Reverend Bryan K. Litton, pastor of First Baptist Church of Jefferson Gardens, was charged with nine counts of forgery involving checks drawn on the church's bank account. If convicted, he faces up to 72 years in prison. The church members, though shocked, are still supporting him and have voted 21-3 to keep him as pastor.[1] This changed in November 1999 when he was arrested again for illegally cashing more church checks while out on bail. In the spring of 2000, he pleaded guilty to four counts of theft and was sentenced to four years in jail and four years probation. He must also make restitution.[2]

In May 1999, Rabbi Jacob Lustig, age 72, admitted stealing from his Cincinnati congregation by skimming proceeds from instant bingo games. He was spared a prison term when he was ordered to forfeit more than $920,000, surrender his passport, and perform community service as part of his sentencing in the Ohio Hamilton County Common Pleas Court. The sale of instant bingo scratch-off cards took in more than $1 million for 1996 and 1997, but his Kneseth Israel Congregation received only $25,000.[3]

These religious institutions lost thousands of dollars and were faced with a credibility problem. Even casual reviews of quarterly, biannual, or annual record keeping could have prevented the opportunity for the theft. When opportunity is coupled with motive and there is no audit, the embezzler has free reign.

In one church, the treasurer handled several hundred thousand dollars a year. While there was no indication that she ever used the money for personal gain, she nevertheless was "free" with the usage of the money. She bought an expensive piano for the church, but presented it as if it were a contribution to the church from her family, while the "gift" was entirely church funded.[4]

A lifetime member of this congregation, the treasurer also chose to be benevolent in other ways. As a member of the wedding committee, she would often give thousands of dollars away to brides-to-be in order that they might have their dream wedding. But the money she allocated wasn't her money—it was taken from the church treasury. When the auditors finally completed their accounting, over $500,000 had been taken. Remarkably, no arrests or prosecutions were made—the church absorbed the loss—but let someone else serve as treasurer.[5]

In Mississippi, casino gambling was voted in a number of years ago. Church treasurers with gambling addictions have defrauded at least eight Baptist churches.[6] The co-authors have not interviewed other denominational leaders to determine the intensity of this problem. While the treasurers probably intended to repay the money, the gambling was too much of a lure. The church lost the money, the treasurers lost their reputations and sometimes their freedom as some were sentenced to prison.

Major denominations once listed individual church giving amounts on a year-to-year basis. However, that approach is now unacceptable. The easiest way for a treasurer or any other leader in a position of trust to "cheat" the budget is on missions offering money.[7] They must pay the utility bills and they should pay the insurance bill. Some are telling the church that they are giving a specific amount of money to missions or individual missionaries, but they send about one-half the stated amount and pocket the remainder. Only when you get the published denominational contributions can you see the misrepresentation. To combat this possibility, many denominations publish their mission giving statements quarterly, or at least at six-month intervals.[8]

Embezzlement can happen very easily. The pastor, priest, or rabbi who writes checks to himself is perfectly entitled to use the checkbook. However, he is not entitled to forge someone's signature. Staff members associated with religious work are often underpaid and they, too, share the American dream—making money to secure their future.

After a congregation has been victimized, it must admit to the mistakes that were made. Denial will keep a congregation from examining current policies and finding ways to prevent these types of crimes. You must admit that the proper checks and balances were not in place and you must find a way to prevent such crimes from occurring again. For example, requiring two signatures on a check and having a third party maintain the checkbook could eliminate forgery, unless the checkbook holder decides to shop. Regular audits by another bookkeeper or an accountant ensure that all expenditures are legitimate. Financial statements should be provided to the membership on a regular basis and, if necessary, published.

When questionable activities (such as the above examples) occur at your facility, you must be careful not to let friendship or collegiality stand in the way of an official police investigation. Often these cases involve multiple agencies and interstate operations. Therefore, you will experience investigative delays. Much of the information will be vague, but put together may articulate criminal activity. In our research we never found a single case that was dismissed or proven false. Accounting errors do occur, but when the discrepancies add up to large sums, you are probably looking at a crime instead of sloppy bookkeeping.

Con men target churches, mosques, synagogues, and temples to defraud the institution, selling investment schemes for idle accounts, or to target the congregation by getting individuals to invest in unique ways—normally high risk investments. But there are many cons and many approaches used by con artists.

Conning Is a Way of Life

In February 1997, four Kentuckians were sentenced for embezzling a Matewan church in Hunting, West Virginia, out of nearly $200,000 in a classic pyramid scheme. John Holtzclaw, age 60, was convicted of one count of conspiracy, two counts of interstate transportation of money obtained by fraud and three counts of money laundering and was ordered to serve 41 months in prison followed by three years of supervised release. Three other individuals were convicted of conspiracy and interstate transportation of money, obtained by fraud. Sentences for the three ranged from 12 to 24 months in prison and three years of supervised release, plus making restitution.

According to prosecutors, the four involved the First Assembly of God of Matewan in a scheme that focused on the sale of gold coins. Pyramid schemes rely on a continual supply of new investors, who are asked to find others to participate. But as the number of new investors dwindles, the money dries up and late participants lose money. The defendants were ordered to reimburse the Matewan church a total of $134,905.[9]

A Des Moines-based Open Bible Standard church and an undisclosed number of Iowa members were among investors in a company allegedly bilked of at least, $5.2 million, according to a Federal grand jury. The indictment, issued in December 1992, portrayed the Open Bible pastor in Custer, South Dakota, as the kingpin in the scheme. He faced seven counts of conspiracy, mail fraud, wire fraud, and money laundering. Open Bible Standard churches are a Pentecostal denomination with 46,000 members in about 350 churches. Their general superintendent, Reverend Ray Smith, said, "We are not convinced this is a scam. If the courts prove that to be true, we will be among the most disappointed.[10] While we do not know the trial outcome, numerous articles were published and reputations were tarnished as a result of this incident.

Con games are a way of life for many people. These crooks go from city to city, house to house, and religious organization to religious organization conning victims out of money. Perhaps you have read newspaper accounts of individuals who have lost thousands of dollars on home repair scams or "pigeon drops." Door-to-door sales representatives have been known to offer a product for sale or have solicited money for a charitable event, only to cash the checks and disappear.

Individuals wearing bright smiles and professional clothing prey on victims who are trusting. These articulate crime professionals make their living by conning people out of money. Their ability to charm people often provides them with a luxurious lifestyle. It is sad that con artists are increasingly targeting religious institutions.

Charity Scams

Unworthy individuals often approach a church, asking for money for gas or food. After convincing the pastor or a staff member of their pressing need, they take the money and buy drugs or alcohol or spend it on other selfish priorities. Additionally, con artists have discovered that they can "earn" more money if they ask for rent money. "My children and I are going to be kicked out of our apartment today! And me with no job." To sound legitimate, they ask you to write a church check to their landlord, rather than themselves. But the "landlord" could be their crime partner, so this needs to be considered.

Some cons will even give you a phone number so that you can call their "landlord" and verify the information. After you call their "landlord," they are out of town with your money. When you call to verify a "tale of woe" be sure to use the telephone number recorded in the phonebook, not a number given by a person requesting assistance. That way, you can ensure that you call the correct person. If you feel uncomfortable doing this, then go to another office or let another staff member make the necessary calls as you continue your pre-funding charity interview.

If a person is requesting money for a utility bill, ask to see the bill. If you decide to pay the bill, write the check directly to the utility company and mail the check yourself. Do not give the money or the check for the bill to the individual.

Repair Scams

Additionally, con artists often offer to contract for needed repairs. These "repair scams" are especially likely to occur after a major fire or natural disaster. Some cons approach a religious organization and offer to clean the gutters, repair the roof, or cut the grass. They will usually ask for a percentage of their pay before beginning the work so that they can purchase the materials for the job. After obtaining the payment, however, they never return. In some instances, the individual may return and begin the work. However, within a few hours, they discover something else that needs to be repaired. They then ask for additional money to purchase the materials for the new repair. After obtaining the additional money, they take your materials and leave, never to return.

How Can Religious Organizations Avoid Victimization?

Always investigate the request for assistance or the offer of a sale for products or services. If you are planning to employ a contractor, you should check local references and consider the advantages of hiring a local contractor. You will be able to locate the contractor if something should go wrong. Co-author Quarles recently employed a contractor to install carpet in his church sanctuary. Since local contractors were not competitive in terms of installation per square foot, a church committee searched the state denominational newspaper and found a contractor who had worked with several churches successfully. The committee chairman checked the business references prior to hiring the contractor. This resulted in a "hassle-free" project because of the references and the background inquiry.

Pay the Supplier Yourself Whenever Possible

Additionally, it is important to obtain a notarized "Contractors Affidavit and Waiver of Material Liens" after a construction job has been completed. This is a waiver from the contractor stating that all subcontractors have been paid and that all suppliers have been paid. This protects your congregation from having liens placed on the property if the contractor does not pay his bills. In a recent case, a local church hired a contractor to build and complete a large gymnasium. When the building was complete, the church treasurer paid the contractor. Several months later, the sheriff's department served the church with a "Material Lien" warrant. The church was being sued because the contractor had not paid his bill to one of his primary material suppliers. The church thought they were debt-free until they were presented with this invoice.[11]

The best option is probably for the church treasurer to pay all of the material bills. The contractor's service and labor bill can be handled separately. This just helps keep everybody honest. You never know when a business is near bankruptcy. If they go to court, the company's assets are seized, and the court pays. But this is amortized. Percentages are paid to all invoices. The money you just paid will not be transferred to "your" vendors, rather it is divided in an equitable court-approved fashion. The end result is the same, however. Your religious institution goes to court, and you are double-billed for some goods and services.

Religious Cons

Cons claiming affiliation with religious groups or missionary and humanitarian organizations conduct another type of con game. Congregational members have been conned into donating money from their savings and retirement accounts for church work, only to discover that the money was never deposited into the coffers of the intended organization. The person who received the donation skipped town. Additionally, congregational members have donated thousands of dollars to limited partnerships in a time-share residential program only to have the program go bankrupt losing all of their money.

Church members have donated money to independent missionaries only to discover that no such program existed. Many churches support or partially support independent missionaries and mission efforts. Increasingly, we risk being victimized in mission scams as we support such efforts. The authors are not suggesting that you stop your support of independent efforts. We are suggesting that you check into all details to ensure your monies are being spent appropriately.

When you give to well-established mission organizations, you are assured that the monies go to the field where it is needed the most. Some 10 to 15 percent of these monies are used for mission organization administrative costs, but the long established groups are usually creditable. However, you do need to look at their annual financial reports. If administrative costs are excessive or if the mission organization is encumbered with bureaucratic expenses, perhaps you should consider another mission—one whose administrative costs are more reasonable.

There have also been cases where the pastor, priest, rabbi, treasurer, or bookkeeper was a thief. The first fraud, in these instances, is in conning the congregation into employing them or giving them a non-salaried responsibility. They play the "honesty" role, only to gain the trust of the membership. Then, when the timing is right and there is enough money available to make the theft worthwhile, they make their move. Individuals have been charged with embezzling thousands of dollars throughout the country.

Crimes committed by church members and leaders create a new dilemma because the congregation or its leadership must decide if they are going to prosecute. Sometimes the person will remain in the congregation and ask forgiveness, thereby avoiding prosecution. Some agree to repay the money. Other times, the person leaves town. But whatever the case, the congregation is often hesitant to press charges. Most religious organizations want to avoid the negative press and to avoid the implication that the church is not carefully monitoring and auditing its money, its staff, or its procedures. Criminologists favor prosecution and this would be our recommendation to you, as difficult as it may seem.

As a religious organization, it is important that your employees and those in leadership positions are aware of your policy to prosecute. If someone commits a crime, it should be reported and charges should be pressed. This will keep other congregations from being victimized as the person moves his or her membership.

Cheating Through the Kids

Religious organizations owning and administering kindergartens and schools have reported cases in which the parents have asked for scholarships for tuition, books, etc., because they could not afford to pay. In most cases, the requests are sincere. However, in some cases there is fraud. Parents have solicited money for summer camps and trips for their children when in actuality the parent had money to pay for the activity, choosing instead to con the unsuspecting membership into footing the bill.

Investment Cons

How can we ensure that our organizational investments are not enriching the lives of those who are less than honorable? As with any investment, we should make wise decisions.

1. If dealing with real estate, obtain a certified surveyor's report and a copy of the deed. Have a lawyer review these documents. Co-author Quarles' church purchased lands out of an estate. We assumed the lawyer had done his job, but when the bank wouldn't loan us money for a building on that property, we had to get a quit claim deed from family members. We had "owned" the property for eight years.

2. If donating to any independent mission or to any independent missionary, make certain that the missionaries and their organization are "recognized" by local churches. If your monies are supporting an independent mission, you should confirm if it "really" has a health care, educational, or evangelical training program.

3. If donating to a needy family, it is your responsibility to ensure that the money is used wisely. Develop an application for assistance and investigate the claim to ensure that the money is needed for assistance. This way, you can make referrals to other local programs to assist with bills such as electric, telephone, etc.

The days of taking up an offering for someone and handing them large sums of money are probably over. You must proceed with caution to ensure that true needs are being met. Never give large sums of money spontaneously. If at all possible, investigate the request thoroughly. Make certain that there is a need. Also, donating the money may not be the answer. Many communities have programs available to help individuals who are having financial difficulties. Become familiar with the social services agencies and community action agencies.

Your community may have a printed directory of the services that are available. For example, in Louisville, Kentucky, there is a civic social service program to pay utility bills and phone bills. There are programs to replace furnaces or water heaters for the needy. There are temporary living quarters for individuals who do not have a place to stay. In many cities, these are not shelters. They are apartments or hotel rooms that are available on a temporary basis until the person has an opportunity to meet with social service workers and make permanent arrangements. Additionally, many of these programs will run a background report through the police department to ensure that this person is not running from the law. Be very cautious if a person tells you that he or she cannot stay at a temporary living quarter. That statement could be a key to the fact that this person does not want a record check.

Combining your outreach and benevolent programs with the services available in the community will help to ensure that more needs are met. This way, you will be able to follow-up with individuals and work with them on their spiritual needs while not draining your financial resources. We want to help individuals who need help; however, with the skills of the con artists, it is challenging to distinguish between the truly needy and the truly greedy. Proceed with caution.

Endnotes

1. Gregory A. Hall, "Church Loss to Gambling Is $11,000: Pastor Held," *Louisville* (Ky.) *Courier Journal*, 25 June, 1999, pp. A1 and A14.

2. Ben Z. Hershbert, "Ex-Indiana Pastor Admits He Stole," *Louisville* (Ky) *Courier Journal, n.p.*

3. Associated Press, "Rabbi Who Stole Won't Be Jailed," *Louisville* (Ky) *Courier,* May 1999, n.p.

4. Dr. John Paul Jones, former director of the Christian Action Commission, Mississippi Baptist Convention Board, interview by author, January 2001.

5. To prevent secondary victimization to both the church and the perpetrator, the co-authors are maintaining confidentiality in reference to this event. However, we have heard of similar events in other states, in other denominations, and in other churches. While an exception, this is not unheard of. This is the case of the "altruistic" thief.

6. Dr. John Paul Jones, former director of the Christian Action Commission, Mississippi Baptist Convention Board, interview with authors, January 2001.

7. Ibid.

8. Ibid.

9. *Louisville* (Ky.) *Courier Journal*, "Four Kentuckians Sentenced in Pyramid Scheme," 4 February, 1997, n.p.

10. William Simbro, "Churches May Have Been Bilked," *Des Moines* (Iowa) *Register*, 7 February, 1993, n.p.

11. A confidential source in north Mississippi.

Part III:
Protecting People

CHAPTER 9

Robbery

It was a typical Wednesday night in rural Knox County in Eastern Kentucky. The small congregation of the Liberty Missionary Baptist Church had just gathered to worship. As pastor John Laws was leading the service, a man dressed in black, wearing both a ski mask and sunglasses, barged into the front door. From the pulpit, pastor Laws watched in horror as the man demanded money from everyone inside.[1] In less than five minutes, the robber moved up and down the aisle, ordering members of the congregation to drop their wallets or purses into a black gym bag. Before he left, he warned members not to follow him or to call for help immediately. He grossed approximately $400.

The Riverside Baptist Church in Nashville, Tennessee, was robbed on a "Mission Emphasis Night." The intruder entered the church, grabbed the pastor's wife and while holding a knife at her throat, robbed the entire congregation.[2]

In North Hollywood, California, a robber and two accomplices entered a weekday evening service, shooting one worshiper in the arm and side. The robbers then stole money, jewelry, and car keys from the attending members.[3]

The Reverend W. Douglas Ensminger, senior minister of Central Presbyterian Church in Houston, Texas, reported that in August 1990, 24 members of a night study class were robbed at gunpoint.[4] After this incident, the church hired an evening guard and closed two entrances to the church.

On October 2, 1994, in Chicago, Illinois, a man wearing a ski mask entered a small church in downtown Chicago immediately after the morning offering was collected. He grabbed an elderly woman sitting on the back row, put a straight razor to her throat and demanded the offering. The robber fled on foot with approximately $100.[5]

In February 1991, in Golden, Colorado, five men entered a church and robbed 32 parishioners at gunpoint. One of the robbers fired a shotgun at one member, ultimately causing the victim's leg to be amputated. The suspects were arrested in Colby, Kansas, after they were stopped for speeding. The suspects were believed to be associated with Asian gangs operating in cities such as Los Angeles, Houston, Salt Lake City, and Kansas City.[6]

In January 1995, the pastor of Saint Savior in Park Slope, New York, was taking the Sunday collection to the bank. He was hit in the back of the head and was hospitalized because of his injuries.[7]

What Is a Robbery?

In most states a robbery is generally defined as the "taking of property by force or violence, (or the threat of force or violence), with the intent to permanently deprive." A weapon is often used. The attack is called a "strong-arm" robbery if no weapon is used. Sometimes the robbery leads to assault and murder. More people are murdered during robberies than rapes, burglaries, or other criminal actions. J. Edgar Hoover, the founding director of the FBI said, "Robbery is death looking for a place to happen."

Vulnerability Indicators

- When offerings are counted.
- When the cash is transferred to the bank.
- When the cash is kept overnight.

With all crime, time is an important commodity. How much time does it take to get in, get out, and complete the robbery? What are the risks? What are the benefits? In a bank robbery, the robber tries to complete the crime in less than 180 seconds, predicting a silent alarm and a police response as a normal probability. In a house of worship robbery, an alarm is unlikely. However, the robber must consider the number of victims and the potential for danger.

He still wants to get in and get out with a high return and a low risk for his crime. Smaller facilities are more likely to be robbed because of the fewer number of people, easy cash, and a receptive audience. Robbing more than one person at a time obviously produces more benefits than the attack on an individual. Larger worship audiences may also include armed plainclothes police officers and these facilities may have more security provisions in place.

While all robbers want money, many are desperate. Some are drug addicts and need money to purchase drugs or pay their supplier. If an addict is in arrears on his drug account, he is likely to be beaten severely, kneecapped, or even killed. This isn't Hollywood, this is reality throughout the American drug culture.

Robbers choose targets because of the "ease" with which they can commit the crime. A church, mosque, synagogue, or temple is usually ideal. No cameras! No weapons! No dogs! Members are less likely to carry a gun than the average citizen on the street. The question no longer is "Why?" The question becomes "Why not?" For religious facilities, the question "Why not more often?" is appropriate.

The robbery becomes more dangerous as the time factor increases. Each second increases the likelihood of arrest and capture. The most dangerous time during a robbery, however, is when the police arrive and the perpetrator is still at the scene. In this case, an individual is often taken hostage, usually a compliant female. Occasionally, the group is held captive in what authorities call a "barricade hostage situation." The robber holds all of your members at gunpoint.

A robbery is incredibly dangerous. It is also very dangerous to distract a robber. You don't know how desperate or how angry the criminal is. To increase your chances of survival, you should cooperate and help the robber succeed. When he is gone, the threat of violence is over as well. We have many accounts of robberies committed inside religious facilities and outside religious facilities including before, during, and after services. Everyone from entire congregations, pastors, and individuals were robbed. The examples could go on for pages and would ultimately cover almost every religion and denomination represented in the United States.

Most of the material in this book is based on contemporary crime prevention approaches. However, in the religious community, many believers want to understand what the Bible, Torah, and the Hebraic scriptures say about these matters. There are very few examples of specific robbery prevention tactics mentioned in these materials. However, many of the military attacks were also criminal, because the Israelites were taken hostage, their assets seized, and their food supplies taken. When Nehemiah was re-building the walls and the temple at Jerusalem, his enemies "conspired together to come to fight against Jerusalem and to hinder it."[8] Nehemiah, the "project administrator" reacted.

These scriptures also reflect some options for the contemporary church. *They prayed and they "set a watch."* Now the Israelites didn't have modern weapons. Archers and javelin throwers are limited to very close ranges. The watch that occurred was basically a lookout, a very good practice for modern houses of worship experiencing crime or the threat of crime.

> **Hebraic Scriptures**
>
> Nevertheless we made our prayer unto our God, and set a watch against them day and night, because of them.—Neh. 4:9 (AV)

Where Do Robberies Occur?

Robbery may occur at any place and at any time. Your protection lies in your overall building security program, or, if robbed, in your ability to remain calm. As the robbers look in your eyes and threaten your life, you must remain calm. During a congregational robbery, each member may be robbed of cash, wallets, jewelry, and car keys. Sometimes the robber may simply demand the offering plates or the poor boxes. Congregational robberies may be the most dangerous, both for you and for the robber. The congregational robbery takes more time and there are more witnesses. The predators must also consider the potential for someone to play hero. It is a good idea to consider this option within your security program as well. Robbery may also occur in the counting rooms, office, or while transporting the money.

Additionally, robbers may enter the sanctuary and demand the offering plates. This is an easier crime to commit, but less lucrative than robbing each individual because the criminal foregoes the jewelry and the cash remaining in worshiper's wallets. We believe that smaller congregations are more susceptible to congregational robberies. While we do not have scientific data to support this observation, it is our belief that the size of the congregation may determine the risk/benefit factors. If a robber can walk in and gather 18 to 20 wallets and jewelry in a few minutes, it would be a decent haul. If a robber walks in and collects the offering plate from a large congregation, that, too, would be a successful crime venture. However, in considering the risk, the larger the congregation, the more likely a robber is to encounter resistance and possibly be followed upon leaving.

Possible Locations for Robbery

We have many examples of congregations being robbed in the sanctuary and examples of robberies in small classroom and wedding settings. Additionally, we have cases where members have been robbed while in the process of sorting and counting the offerings. For example, in April of 1993 the Easter offering plate was piled high with more than $7,000 in checks, bills, and change—all destined for charities—until an intruder stole nearly $1,200 in cash from the offering plate when the volunteer counter left the room for a moment.[9] Robbers have hidden in "counting rooms" while waiting for the money to be transferred from the sanctuary. They have hidden outside the building awaiting the transfer to a bank. Criminals have identified the individuals transporting the money and wait for an opportunity to rob them while en route versus robbing them at the bank, where cameras are generally installed.

It is not unusual for robbery to occur with pastors, staff, and volunteers as victims. It is more likely to happen at any time when someone is *working alone* in your facility. Females have been robbed—and since they are alone—raped, as well. Pastors, priests, and rabbis have been assaulted and robbed by individuals requesting aid or counsel. Females have been assaulted, robbed, and raped as they walked to their cars or homes.

Who Are the Robbers?

Young people seem to be the primary robbers today. Available statistics indicate that almost three-fourths of all robbers are under the age of 25, that slightly over half of all robbers are under the age of 21, and that almost one-third are under the age of 18. Nearly 10 percent are women.[10]

When Do Religious Facility Robberies Occur?

We do not have enough specific information on robberies in houses of worship to give a prediction of when robbery is more likely to occur. However, we know that it generally occurs when the facility is vacant, or when most worshipers have departed the premises. The criminal plans his attack around the availability of victims, the vulnerability of victims, and his opportunity to catch them alone. Based on this crime knowledge, we can make more educated assessments on "when" they are most likely to strike.

> **Robberies Most Like Occur When**
>
> - Victims are available.
> - Victims are vulnerable.
> - Victims are alone.

Additionally, church members are vulnerable to robbery when transporting the money from the church to the bank. Since criminals often identify the money-carrier and rob them while en route, it is recommended that you alternate the persons making the deposit and that a second or even a third car, preferably equipped with cellular phones, be used for making non-banking hour deposits. Special care should be taken after night service offerings. Some facilities even use armed couriers and armored vehicles to transport large Sunday morning offerings.

The time frame studies indicate that there are more nighttime robberies than daytime robberies in or around religious facilities, so inferentially, your risk is greater after an evening service offering, than for the morning worship period. Darkness is a friend of the robber. This is another reason to invest in effective lighting systems.

We don't have a profile on inside church robberies and admittedly these are rare occurrences. However, we can indicate, through one of the largest robbery studies ever completed in the continental United States, what the street, parking lot, and outside robbery crimes against individuals and individual families are.[11] We can then be even more wary—and more careful during these times.

What Is an Armed Robbery Like?

Robbery is quick, decisive, and ruthless. The robber wants to gain control quickly and establish his influence. Normally, this is done with death threats and shouts of

What to Do Should An Armed Robbery Occur

- Cooperate.
- Do exactly what the robber demands.
- Help the robber get in and out as quickly as possible.
- Don't speak unless ordered to.
- Don't debate or argue.
- Don't move unless you are directed to.
- Don't do anything you are not ordered to do.
- If the robber tells you to lie down or stay seated for five or 10 minutes, then do so.
- Remember: Lives are more important than cash or jewelry.

profanity. According to the Bureau of Justice Statistics, 71 percent of all "arrested" robbers are under the age of 25. That would indicate that the average robber is young, quick, and strong. The robber may think that he can successfully rob a large number of worshipers and survive. He may be willing to take the risk. He is certainly willing to use the force necessary to succeed and once a robbery has started, there is no turning back. If the robber is under the influence of alcohol or drugs, the risk for violence may spiral out of control.

How to Avoid Injuries and Death During a Robbery

Any crime is difficult. The victim may overreact or underreact, increasing his or her risk. Every victim should maintain composure and self-control. While armed robbers are frightening, fewer victims are injured in armed robberies than in unarmed robberies.[12] Only 0.2 percent of these robberies resulted in murder. These national statistics, however, apply to robberies against individuals. The group robbery, as in a church, provides many more risks. This is where a pastor, priest, rabbi, minister, or lay speaker can help save lives by being a calming influence on the congregation. He or she can ask the congregation to remain calm and to stay seated, and ask the robber if it is all right to pray. Even if the robber says, "no," silent prayers should go up at that moment.

What You Can Do

There are several precautionary steps that you can take to reduce the potential of robbery in your facility. As mentioned throughout the book, good lighting and security procedures are key to your success. However, since a robber is after cash, we offer additional suggestions.

First, it is recommended that offerings be counted in a secure room with a strong (solid core or steel) door. A peephole should be installed. An inexpensive one with a strong lock and deadbolt is less than $10 at a local hardware store. A quality peephole with excellent visibility can be purchased for less than $50. These peepholes measure about two-and-a-half inches in diameter. Additionally, in larger churches, mosques, synagogues, and temples you should station a "guardian" outside the counting room door to serve as a lookout in the event someone decides to enter uninvited. In large churches you may even place someone in another room, but in view of the guardian outside the door. If the guardian is threatened or overpowered, the person in the other room can call 911 or come to his assistance.

The counting room should be equipped with a telephone, a foot switch, and hand activated robbery alarm duress button. This must be a silent alarm. Police authorities are trained in how to respond to a robbery of this type. The foot switch enables you to activate the alarm and camera system surreptitiously. Your motion is hidden and does not come to the robber's attention. It is important to activate the switch immediately because every second he is there increases your risk.

If finances are available, we encourage the use of CCTV. You may choose to publicize this protection, hanging signs in common areas that the cameras are recording. Simply mounting a camera facing the entry doors of the worship center and of the offering counting room is good crime prevention. Many robbers may choose to steal elsewhere.

On the average, the armed robber is alone. Usually, he will show a weapon and quietly tell you that you are being held up. If you are still in the counting room, it would be ideal to hit a silent alarm. After hitting the alarm and camera foot switch, you should immediately begin to comply with the robber's instructions. Keep your hands in plain view at all times. If he tells you to give him the money, do so carefully and release the money, moving your hands slowly with the palms faced out, so that he sees you are not a threat and that you have no weapon. Don't offer to get additional money from the safe or a cash drawer. This overcompliance increases the amount of time the armed predator remains on your premises. Your goal is to help him leave as quickly as possible. The faster you can get him out safely, the better. Telling him that there is another $30,000 in the safe is not the appropriate reaction.

As long as he remains, continue to face him. Observe his eyes and facial expression. However, do not appear to be studying him as this could make him nervous. By observing his facial features, you may be able to predict if he is going to start shooting. Look for clues, but without staring. Listen to his grammar, accent, and voice. Listen for word distinctions. Try to notice his eyes and expressions. You should also notice height, weight, skin color, lips, eye color, as well as blemishes, scars, marks, and tattoos. If he has a crime partner, listen to how he addresses the partner. You may be able to pick up clues that will aid police investigators.

Once the money requested has been handed over, place your hands in plain view and remain quiet. You don't want him to still be in the building when the police arrive because this could result in a hostage situation or a shoot-out. Lock the door behind him as soon as he leaves. Stay there until the police arrive or until someone comes to get you.

If the situation should result in a "shoot-out," the best plan is to *get on the floor quickly*. At the very least, you should remain seated. If you can crawl under a desk, pew, or alter table, do so. However, if you've been told not to move, you should follow those directions, especially if you are within view of the robber. Only you can determine if the robber intends to use his weapon.

We encourage you to comply with the robber's instructions. Let him know that you intend to cooperate fully. However, we don't want you to *overcomply* any more than we want you to resist. Since the robber is usually only interested in money, we believe cooperation is to your benefit. We do not recommend cooperation or compliance when the robber wants you to walk out of the facility door with him or to get in his car. There are additional crimes that are likely to occur if you comply with these requests. Assault, kidnapping, rape, and murder are among them. Robbery survival is probably the easiest of the alternatives.

If you are taken hostage at gunpoint, you should still do what the robber instructs. A man could reasonably expect to be released. A woman has a real problem because the robber is usually an all-encompassing predator, and he may attempt rape. You may choose to feign fainting—although this won't be hard—you really will be scared. Certainly you won't want to leave with him. If you are taken hostage, remember that the police will not endanger your life just to apprehend him. Don't endanger your life by foolish actions.[13]

Final Recommendations

To prevent robbery against individuals or from money rooms, we recommend that you always have more than one person present. This is also helpful when pastors, priests, and rabbis are asked to counsel individuals they don't know. When witnessed by others, both crime and the potential for abusive gossip are eliminated. If a predator has scheduled a counseling session for less than honorable reasons, you will have deterred that risk. Many counselors have been assaulted and robbed when alone in their offices studying or preparing to counsel.

If you are robbed, we encourage you to cooperate fully. Someone who is in close proximity with a weapon has already made you a victim. Don't add other risks to this equation. Assault, rape, and murder can occur as the intensity of the event spirals. Again, we *do not recommend cooperation* if the robber wants you to walk out of the church door with him or get in his car. Additional crime threats are revealed at this time.

There is no recommendation that will protect you in every situation. However, complying, talking, singing, praying, or fainting are viable distractions. Listen to your inner voice. Proceed with extreme caution. Never leave with your perpetrator because your chances for survival are greatly reduced if you do.

Endnotes

1. Joyce Sweeney Martin, "Gunman Robs Wednesday Night Worshipers," *Lexington Herald-Leader*, February 14, 1997, p. 3. Gail Gibson, "Stand and Deliver: Robber Holds up Congregation, *Lexington Herald-Leader,* January 24, 1997, A-1 and A-6.

2. Michael Burns, an associate pastor in the Riverdale Baptist Church in Nashville, TN, on November 15, 2000. An interview by the author confirmed story. This event occurred during the late 1970s or the early 1980s, affirming the long-standing history of criminal attacks against churches in America.

3. Tina Daunt, "Violence Enters Churches' Doors," *Los Angeles* (Ca.) *Times*, 9 November, 1993, n.p.

4. Richard Vars, "Crime Fears Taking Toll On Ministry," *Houston* (Tex.) *Chronicle*, 17 August, 1990, n.p.

5. Paula Ratliff, co-author, and Burnie Mixon, staff writer for the *Chicago Tribune*. Telephone conversation on October 9, 1994.

6. Bruce Finley, "Asians Suspected in Rash of Crimes," *Denver* (Colo.) *Post*, 23 February, 1991, n.p.

7. Annette Fuentes, "Churches Not Sacred to Thieves," *New York Daily News*, 8 January, 1995, n.p.

8. Neh. 4:8, Authorized (King James) Version.

9. Laurie Goldstein, "No Longer a Sanctuary From Crime," *The Washington Post*, 4 June, 1993, n.p.

10. U.S. Department of Justice, Uniform Crime Reports, *Crime in the United States*, (Washington D.C.: U.S. Government Printing Office),1998, p. 17.

11. U.S. Department of Justice, Law Enforcement Assistance Administration, *Police Robbery Control Manual,* 1975.

12. John M. MacDonald, *Armed Robbery* (Springfield, Illinois: Charles C. Thomas, Publisher, 1975), p. 139.

13. B.I. Ehrstine and J.A. Mack, *Profitability Through Loss Control* (Cincinatti: Anderson Publishing Company, 1977), p. 91.

CHAPTER 10

SEX CRIMES

It was just an average church in a nice community in a locale enjoying remarkable demographic and economic growth. It wasn't your church, but it could have been. With a membership of over 250, the church was growing and the fellowship was prospering. Only about six years old, the church was built on the edge of town where new subdivisions were being developed. The church had a comprehensive program with services on Sunday morning, Sunday evening, and Wednesday night in addition to choir practice and men's, women's, youth, and children fellowship groups meeting at other times. The church had an "open door" policy during all services, making it convenient for all worshipers to have full access to any part of the facility.

The church building is shaped like an inverted "L," with the sanctuary forming the central unit and the educational building abutting its back wall. The church offices are on the far end of the first floor, adjacent to a parking lot entrance. The nursery occupies the space across the hall from the church offices. Nursery services are always available during services.

On one rainy winter night, attendance ebbed. Normally, two ladies supervised the nursery department during night services, but because there were only four children there that night, the nursery superintendent urged her co-worker to go out and attend the service. On this night the stranger came in—the rapist, that is. The youth choir singing and the accompanying instruments covered up the nursery superintendent's cries for help as this predator forced her into an adjacent classroom and raped her.[1]

Simple Security Prevention Approaches

1. Environmental Security Issues
- Move the nursery as close to the sanctuary as possible.

2. Church Policy Issues
- Lock the education building doors after church services begin. Install inside panic bars to expedite spontaneous evacuation during an emergency.
- Mandate the 2-plus rule—requiring that two workers (at a minimum) be present with the children. This decreases the chance of victimization by 67 percent. If three or more adult guardians are present the likelihood of criminal activity is decreased by 90 percent.[2]

As horrible as this attack was, it was probably avoidable. It could have been deterred, with just a little forethought on the part of church leaders or the security committee.

In another incident, a lady was attacked after the regular service. "The church was empty at the time," said Detective Sergeant Denny Crowe of the Owensboro (Kentucky) Police Department as he released the account of a 38-year-old woman who was assaulted, raped, and robbed shortly after a noon Sunday service.[3] The victim had remained for a period of private reflection and prayer after the congregation left and was attacked from behind. Despite a jaw broken in two places, the woman checked herself out of the county hospital and spent the day with a police artist working on a sketch of the suspect. That was September 11, 1995. The case is still unsolved.

We have many reports of church secretaries and volunteers being raped while the pastor, priest, or rabbi was running errands. In Indiana, an 18-year-old delinquent attacked a ten year old girl, dragged her behind the church, and raped her.[4] A woman was raped in a church in Washington, D.C., and a nun in Baltimore was strangled when she surprised an early-morning intruder in her convent in March of 1993.[5]

In Dallas, a married missionary lady was raped by a married deacon.[6] Her husband was speaking at one church and she at another. She stayed late, answering questions. The deacon offered to help carry the "mission exhibit" to her van. He attacked her in the parking lot and pushed her into the van. She called the police immediately and the deacon was arrested. She was traumatized. The church's reputation and the deacon's reputation were microscopically examined. Some members of the church didn't believe "their" deacon had raped her. "It just couldn't happen!" It was not until the scientific evidence of seminal fluids was processed for DNA types that the crime laboratory confirmed that this particular deacon had molested her. The evidence proved him to be a liar, for he had publicly stated that he had never even molested her, much less had sex with her.

However, the period between the emergency room evidence kit, the crime lab examination, and the report to the district attorney was lengthy—in fact, it took over six months. During this period, the church faced many difficulties. Some members believed the missionary lady, others believed the deacon. The victim was dealing with the trauma of the rape, the publicity, and the trial. Some church members even wanted to withdraw funding from the missionary couple, as they struggled with this issue.

Perhaps the case would have been more difficult if the deacon had claimed that the union was consensual, but he didn't. He said that he had never behaved inappropriately. The missionary lady had no extensive bruising or black eyes. He simply overpowered her and attacked, thus making the situation even more questionable.

While it is shocking to believe that a rape would occur on religious institution properties, rape is not a new or just a contemporary problem. Probably the first rape was recorded in the 34th chapter of Genesis. This historical account was about a young girl named Dinah, the daughter of Jacob and Leah. The scriptures say that she "went out to see the daughters of the land."[7] When Shechem, the son of Hamor the Hivite saw her, "he took her, and lay with her, and defiled her."[8] A prince of his country, he fell in love with her and asked for a marital arrangement.[9] Simeon and Levi, sons of Jacob and Dinah's brothers sneaked into the city, slew all of the males, and took all of their worldly goods,[10] so the sin and crime of rape ultimately resulted in homicide and disharmony between these peoples.

Rape is the dirtiest four-letter word in the English language. It is one of the most volatile acts and is feared by most, if not all, females. Criminological statistics by the U.S. Department of Justice indicate that at least one in 12 of all females in America will suffer the indignities of rape or attempted rape during her lifetime.[11] The United States has the highest rape *rate* of all the developed countries publishing "reported to police cases."[12] American women are several hundred times more likely to be raped than are women in other countries.[13]

Our rape rate is four times higher than that of Germany, 13 times higher than that of England, and 20 times higher than that of Japan.[14] Some crime studies indicate that the number is as high as one in four of all women. Since as few as one in 12 rapes are even reported, the real statistics indicate a larger and uglier picture. This trend is noticed in other crimes as well, for studies indicate that roughly half of the personal crimes committed in this country are never reported.[15]

More than half of all rapes reported to police are on women under the age of 19.[16] A disproportionate number of victims are attacked before they can legally drive.[17] The rape victim profile usually begins at about 10 years of age and peaks at 16.[18] Because rapists seem to prefer young, inexperienced, and easily intimidated girls, we have an enormous responsibility to maintain a secure environment, especially for our youth. However, it should never be assumed that older women, married women, or widows will not be attacked. A rapist will attack any female who is alone and vulnerable. Age, size, build, and attractiveness are generally not important to a rapist, unless the rapist has some bizarre sexual fetish. Predators attack victims perceived to be weaker than themselves.

Rape Settings

The women in the congregation must be aware of each setting in which they are at risk. This includes work environments, shopping, driving, walking, working at home, or while attending church. Any situation in which a woman is alone creates the potential for victimization. If a woman is comfortable in the setting, she is less likely to be suspicious. Her lack of apprehension increases the risk.

The victim in Owensboro, Kentucky, certainly was not thinking of rape while praying at the church. Yet, the criminal found her and took the opportunity to victimize her. Rapes have often been reported in homes, automobiles, businesses, buses, educational facilities, restaurants, alleys, shopping malls, parking lots, and about every place imaginable, but how often have we considered religious institutions as a "rape place"?

During our research for this book, the co-authors found many incidents of rape in church. Women have been raped in church gardens while tending the flowers. Young girls have been raped in classrooms. A nursery worker was raped *during* church in southern Mississippi.[19] Secretaries have been raped in church facilities. We discovered reports of rapes in rural and urban religious settings, both in large and small houses of worship.

Our goal of this chapter is not to "frighten" women or to keep them from attending services. Rather, our goal is to increase the awareness and to help religious leaders advise women appropriately and to proceed with caution at all times, especially *when they are alone* and in a setting in which there are no security cameras, alarm buttons, or witnesses.

Is Your Facility Vulnerable?

If you have members, especially females, working alone in your complex, then the answer is yes. Your facility is vulnerable. It is recommended that you implement the policy that females *must not* work alone on the premises. This will greatly reduce the potential for rape because 98 percent of all rape victims *are alone* at the time of their attack. There is safety in numbers. Additionally, we recommend that administrators determine the times the building is accessible by anyone. You need to consider if criminals have access to the building at the same time in which your membership is utilizing the premises and determine how many people will be on-site. Addressing items such as how often a secretary is left alone in the building, and responding to that information will reduce the potential for victimization.

Does your religion or denomination educate young adults about the crime of rape, particularly "acquaintance rape?" Do your young people know what to do in the event they are attacked? Have you educated your ministers, pastors, priests, and rabbis on their appropriate role when a member reports a rape to them? We must recognize that many members of our congregations are raped by people whom they are dating, sometimes by those they meet in church.

Co-author Quarles' wife was accosted as a youth in an isolated area of Mississippi's largest church by a boy in her Sunday School department. Sensing her vulnerability and feeling uncomfortable, she ran away, avoiding embarrassment and assault. This incident was never officially reported. Many, perhaps most victims of this crime, fear public knowledge or the notoriety associated with the offense, so they suffer in silence, suffering for the rest of their lives. Some victims even blame themselves for the event. "If I hadn't worn that short skirt or that sweater, I wouldn't have been raped. It's all my fault," they say. But it isn't. Even nuns with the full ecumenical garb are attacked at church. It is the rapist's mind-set, not the victim's dress standard that caused the attack.

> A divorcee with a child met her assailant in the singles Bible Study Class at her church. She thought that it was always "safe" to date guys she met at church. She never thought that a predator would pick his victim at church, but she was wrong.
>
> She doesn't go to that church any more and she is still apprehensive. She doesn't trust men she meets at church anymore. She never reported the event to the police, only to her trauma counselor.[20]

Stranger Rape Versus Date Rape

Many young people, as well as more mature females in your congregation may be raped or sexually assaulted on your property, on trips, or during sponsored activities. Knowledge and awareness about this problem is very important. Whether talking about a street robbery or a rape, there are four stages, as discussed previously. Knowing these stages may give you some more weapons in your "crime prevention tool kit."

The first stage is surveillance. It may last just a few moments or a few days. Criminals select their victims after watching them. If you can detect someone watching you, this is the time to leave quickly. The invitation stage is when you are first approached. He asks an innocuous question, "Can you tell me how to get to the church office?" As he asks, however, he comes closer. The confrontation is when he asks you for your money or your clothes. If he asks for money, throw your purse or wallet past him and run away, screaming all the while. Some authorities call the noise stage, a "power yell." The attack phase is the last. This is when he gets aggressive. Obviously, you will miss it if you get away when you first sense vulnerability during the surveillance stage, or if you run and *power yell* during the confrontation/attack stages after you have thrown away your cash or a small prepared sum of "bait" money.

The observant female can generally deter, avoid, or prevent the attack. However, by the time a rape attempt is initiated, it may be too late to stop it. Rapes are quick, sudden, spontaneous, frightening, and evil. Only about one third of all victims are strong enough to even say no, much less to scream, run away, or otherwise resist.[21]

Only about 12 percent of rape victims try to resist.[22] Only about 12 percent try to run away.[23] The victims are so frightened and so intimidated that they are incapacitated by their fear, even to the point that most of them never even say no, or scream.

The time to avoid a rape is *before it happens*. The first step is to realize that rape can happen to you or to those you love the most. *The woman who denies that anyone would want to rape her is the most likely victim because she won't alter her behavior—or listen to good advice.* "It won't happen to me," she says. Or perhaps she thinks that because she is a "religious" person, God will take care of her and no harm will come to her. Some women deny that they could be a victim because of their physical appearance or because they believe they are too young or too old. This is not the case, however. Co-author Quarles has worked rape cases involving females from the age of infancy and tots on up to an 86-year-old woman raped in a nursing home.

Predators don't think the same way females think. Rapists pick victims who don't think they will be victimized or could be victimized. They pick females who are *alone and vulnerable*. They pick women who are risk takers who don't obey crime prevention rules.

What Should a Victim Do Once the Attack Begins?

If you are confronted by an assailant, get away as soon as you can. If he attempts to restrict you, scream. Don't hesitate to scream as loud as you can because this is the best rape prevention tool. Then you should run as fast as you can and continue screaming. Rape is so scary that few victims fight, but screaming, running, and fighting are the primary rape avoidance approaches.

If you followed the avoidance suggestions but find that you are going to be attacked anyway, our best advice is to talk to the rapist. See if you can learn anything that might help you avoid the attack. Fighting is your last option, unless you believe that you can over-power the rapist. Otherwise you are going to make him madder and the attack even more savage.

If a Rape Occurs at Your Facility

If a rape should occur at your worship complex, report it to your local law enforcement agency immediately. Ensure that the victim is treated at the hospital. Allow the officers the opportunity to question anyone who may be a suspect, even if it means church members must be questioned. If someone in your congregation reports a rape to you, as a minister, pastor, priest, rabbi, or leader, the rape should be reported immediately to the police department *unless the report was given confidentially in a counseling session.* While you should recommend reporting the case to the police, the victim may not want to officially report the crime. Rapists rape again and again and again. By failing to prosecute, they are "enabled" to continue their predatory lifestyle.

If the person accused of committing the rape is a member of your congregation, you will need to address this issue quickly. You still have responsibilities to other potential victims in your membership. The police authorities know how to handle the investigation, but your cooperation will aid them immeasurably.

If the rape occurred on your premises, you incurred a huge liability. You should immediately take steps to ensure that other rapes do not occur. Never assume that this is or was an isolated incident, unlikely to occur again. It just might occur again and it may well have occurred before. Determine where the attack took place. Take proactive steps to ensure that this never happens again. Check the lighting, entranceways, and look for key problems. Why was the area vacant at the time of the attack?

If the rapist is someone in your membership, you must help the congregation deal with the situation. You can't hide an event like this. Avoiding it or hiding it will usually prove unsuccessful. It also increases the liability *and decreases the credibility of your leadership.* Don't make this mistake. You must respond reasonably.

Make it a practice to believe the victim, but be careful not to slander the alleged attacker. Chances are, if a victim claims she was raped, she is sincere. This crime is usually unreported because of the embarrassment and stigmatism associated with the act. We will note that there have been accusations in which there was no rape, but this type of scenario usually involves a family member, i.e., stepfather, stepbrother, etc. You will need to trust your best judgment. However, we would encourage you to involve the police department and to seek a competent investigation.

There is also a civil negligence and liability issue for the congregation, if you do not thoroughly investigate rape and other sexual assault charges. Another rape or sexual assault victim may sue the church for not following through with an official inquiry, for not warning the general membership of the threat, or even for "covering it up—so the church will not be embarrassed." You will need a strong comprehensive insurance policy for your litigation, but you may not have it long. Your insurance policy may be canceled, if your leadership chooses inappropriate responses to this crisis.

Report the crime of rape. Be open and honest with your congregation. Limit the amount of information disclosed to avoid legal actions from the rapist, if the charges are erroneous. Protect the victim's identity, if possible, and ensure that she is counseled. Protect the congregation from future attacks. Act quickly and decisively.

Endnotes

1. The incident referred to was an actual event occurring in a southeastern Protestant church. As in any crime where "secondary victimization" could harm those attacked, the authors choose to refrain from personal, city, or state identifiers.

2. Michael Castelman, *Crime Free,* (New York: Harper & Row Publishers, Inc., 1984), p. 67.

3. Karen Owen, "Church Reclaimed After Rape, " Owensboro (Ky.) *Messenger-Inquirer*, 15 September, 1995, p. 1D.

4. AP Bulletin from Indianapolis, Indiana, "18 Year Old Charged With Raping Girl," Louisville (Ky.) *Courier-Journal*, 7 September, 1994, p. B3.

5. Laurie Goldstein, "No Longer a Sanctuary From Crime," *The Washington Post,* 4 June, 1993, n.p.

6. A missionary lady and her husband, who wish to remain anonymous. Interview by Chester L. Quarles and Bob Klamser, in the mountains of Peru, South America, 1986.

7. Gen. 34:1, Authorized (King James) Version.

8. Gen. 34:2. (AV)

9. Gen. 34:8. (AV)

10. Gen. 34:25-29. (AV)

11. Captain Robert L. Snow, *Protecting Your Life, Home and Property: A Cop Shows You How,* (New York: Plenum Publishing Corporation, 1995), p. 45.

12. The National Victim Center, "Rape Statistics," (Washington, D.C.: The National Victim Center, April 23, 1992).

13. J. L. Simmons and George McCall. *76 Ways to Protect Your Child From Crime,* (New York: Henry Holt and Company, 1992), p. 157.

14. The National Victim Center, "Rape Statistics," (Washington, D.C.: The National Victim Center, April 23, 1992).

15. Morton Bard and Dawn Sangrey, *The Crime Victim's Book* (New York: Basic Books, 1979) p. 161.

16. The National Victim Center and the Crime Victim's Research and Treatment Center, *Rape In America: A Report to the Nation* (Washington, D.C.: U.S. Government Printing Office, 1992).

17. Ibid.

18. Ibid.

19. The authors are concerned about secondary victimization. This event was not documented in the local press, but was discussed in a regional denominational "security" conference. Confidential source interviewed January 2000.

20. The National Victim Center and the Crime Victim's Research and Treatment Center, *Rape In America: A Report to the Nation* (Washington, D.C.: U.S. Government Printing Office, 1992).

21. National Institute of Law Enforcement and Criminal Justice, *Forcible Rape: Police,* vol. I (Washington, D.C.: U.S. Government Printing Office, 1987), p. 19.

22. Ibid.

23. National Victim Center and the Crime Victim's Research and Treatment Center, *Rape In America: A Report to the Nation,* (Washington, D.C., The U.S. Government Printing Office, 1992).

CHAPTER 11

MURDER AND SHOOTINGS

In Waterville, Maine, police arrested a 37-year-old male for beating and stabbing four nuns while they were praying in their convent, the Servants of the Blessed Sacrament, on a Saturday night.[1] He entered the convent by smashing the glass on a locked door. He was not a stranger to the nuns; he often worshiped there with them.

Once inside, he attacked one nun in the chapel and the other three in an adjacent part of the convent. Two of the nuns died due to multiple blunt force injuries to the head. Two nuns were hospitalized in critical condition. They watched in dismay as he bludgeoned one sister with a religious statue. "This may be one of the most heinous crimes ever committed in Maine," said Stephen McCausland, spokesman of the state public safety department.[2]

In Pueblo, Colorado, in August 1996, two priests were found stabbed to death in the church rectory.[3] There was no sign of forced entry. A trail of blood from the rectory indicates the priest struggled with and possibly wounded their attacker. Several days later, a 20-year-old man was arrested and charged with their murder. He was a familiar figure at the church, which was across the street from his home. The news reported that he had spent a month in a psychiatric care unit until just eight months before the murders.[4]

We have reports of numerous shootings in Los Angeles, California:

In 1985, a man shot and killed a pastor and a deacon inside a Chinatown Baptist church. The man, who was a former church member, was fatally shot by an off-duty sheriff's deputy attending the service. In 1986, a man opened fire inside a La Puente Church of Christ. His spray of automatic gunfire killed two church members and wounded two others. In 1987, a bullet splintered the stained glass window of a church and killed a choir member walking down the aisle after rehearsal. In 1989, a gunman burst into the Mt. Olive Church of God in Christ and opened fire on parishioners with a sawed-off shotgun killing two people and injuring one person. In June 1992, two to three gunmen went on a rampage at the St. Agnes Church hall shooting one man and robbing 18 parishioners of their money, jewelry, and car keys. In October 1993, a woman, standing at the altar was shot by two teenagers in a drive-by shooting. The youth open fired through the doors of the sanctuary, critically injuring the woman in the stomach.[5]

In August of 1991, in Phoenix, Arizona, six Buddhist monks and three others were shot and killed at a Buddhist Temple. The bodies were found side by side and indicating that they were kneeling when shot.[6] In July 1993, Jonathan Andrew Doody (age 17 at the time of the murders) was found guilty of nine counts of first-degree murder, nine counts of armed robbery, and one count each of burglary and conspiracy to commit armed robbery.[7] The motive was robbery and "to eliminate the witnesses." Doody had close ties with the Buddhist faith. His mother was a member of the Buddhist temple west of Phoenix and his brother once was a novice monk.

In New Orleans, Louisiana, an associate minister was robbed and gunned down on the church's front lawn beneath a statue of the Virgin Mary.[8] In Bridgeport, Connecticut, a former mayor and two others, including a priest, were critically wounded in a shooting as they stood on the steps of a church.[9] In Palatine, Illinois, a four-year-old boy was stabbed 19 times with a 12-inch knife while staying at the Sikh Religious Society Temple.[10] In North Carolina, a wedding director leaving a Winston-Salem church was stabbed 12 feet from her car. She died at the scene.[11]

On March 11, 1999, in New St. John Fellowship Baptist Church in Gonzales, Louisiana, three people were killed and four were injured.[12] Shon Miller, Sr., at age 22 allegedly killed his mother-in-law, Mildred Vessel. He then went to his wife's church during the Wednesday night service. He first shot two bullets straight up in the air, then told everyone to get down as he headed deliberately to the front in search of his estranged wife. He found her on the fourth row." He killed his wife, Carla Vessel Miller and his son Shon Miller, Jr. Finally, he started shooting at random, killing another parishioner and wounding four others. He calmly stopped to reload in the middle of the killing spree. The suspect was later shot and wounded by police. Church leaders have said that they will never use the building again.[13] On July 3, 1999, at the Korean United Methodist Church in Bloomington, Indiana, one person was killed outside of his church.[14]

On September 15, 1999, at Wedgwood Baptist in Fort Worth, Texas, seven people were killed and seven people were injured when Larry Gene Ashbrook walked up carrying two guns. He opened fire, killing 6 and wounding 8 persons. He then set off a pipe bomb. Hearing the approaching police sirens, he sat down in a pew and killed himself. One of the wounded victims later died in the hospital. Witnesses at the scene stated that the shooter was angrily spouting anti-Baptist rhetoric during the rampage.[15] According to Lana Bull, a seminary student who was lying on the floor next to Kim Jones and within a few feet of the gunman, the last statement of the gunman was, "I'm not interested in y"all, I wanted adults."[16]

How Can We Stop the Murders and Shootings?

Spontaneous killings and group shootings known as "spree killings" are probably the most difficult crimes to deter, much less prevent. Based on the numerous accounts that we have, it would be impossible to tell you how each one could have been prevented. We have encouraged you to install locks, bolts, security alarms, and cameras. We have encouraged you to employ security guards and have a watch committee. We have encouraged you to limit access

> **Viable Prevention Techniques**
>
> • Access protection.
> • CCTV monitoring of property and inside your facility.
> • Uniformed security or police presence stationed outside, on street access areas, and parking areas.
> • Outside welcome committee with cellular phones or radios.
> • Sound room equipped with telephone.
> • Infant nursing rooms equipped with telephone.
> • Outer office space left open and phones available. (It should be mentioned that in several "spree killings, the phones were in locked rooms.)

to your property. However, even with all the precautions, some of these murders could not have been avoided.

Our goal for this chapter is to raise your awareness and cause you to exercise extreme caution. If you begin to utilize some crime prevention techniques as a result of this chapter, then we have been successful. Unless we in America can restore respect for life and respect for religious leaders, it is unlikely that the killings will cease.

The same crime prevention, deterrence, and avoidance approaches that have been recommended in earlier chapters apply here. While it is not an absolute guarantee that these approaches will work in all circumstances, they increase the problems of access and getting away for the criminal. If a perpetrator is determined to commit an offense against a house of worship on a particular occasion, he or she may choose another target as they drive by and see your outside CCTV camera stations, uniformed security personnel, welcoming committee members with radios or cellular phones, and vision "watch" presence at your facility.

If a gunman attempts to bring in a rifle or shotgun, he should be spotted before he reaches the worship center. The reaction to his presence should be to lock the doors and summon the police. While a desperate crime may still be attempted, the likelihood is lessened as the offender fears failure, even if he is not afraid of arrest or death—possibly considering suicide as several spree killers at worship centers have done.

Endnotes

1. Associated Press, "Nuns Killed, 2 Hurt in Convent Attack," *Louisville* (Ky.) *Courier Journal*, 29 January, 1996, n.p.

2. Ibid.

3. Carrie Dowling, "Close-Knit Colorado Town Shaken After Priest Killings," *USA Today*, 9 August, 1996, p. A3.

4. Associated Press, "Suspects in Priests Killing Familiar Figure at Church," Louisville (Ky.) *Courier Journal*, August 1996, n.p.

5. Tina Daunt, "Violence Enters Churches' Doors," *Los Angeles Times*, 9 November, 1993, n.p.

6. Jane Fritsch, "9 Slayings at Temple Baffle Police," *Los Angeles Times*, 12 August, 1991, n.p.

7. Brent Whiting, Pamela Manson, and Karen Kaplan, "Doody Convicted in Temple Slayings," *Phoenix* (Az.) *Republic*, 13 July, 1993, n.p.

8. Mark Schlenfstein, "New Orleans Pastor Slain in Robbery at Church," New Orleans (La.) *Times Picayune*, 29 January, 1994, n.p.

9. J.R. Clark, "Churches Offer Tempting Targets For Crime," John Jay College of Criminal Justice, *Law Enforcement News*, vol. XX, no. 412, 30 November, 1994, p. 5-11.

10. Ray Quintanilla, "Sikhs Might Begin Questioning Visitors After Slaying At Temple," *Louisville* (Ky.) *Courier Journal*, 21 December, 1994, n.p.

11. Jennifer Graham, "Churches Seek Refuge From Crime," [Colombia, S. C.], *State*, 7 December, 1992, n.p.

12. "Violence and Murder in Churches." Available @ ReligiousToleran.org/chu-viol.htm.

13. Ibid.

14. Ibid.

15. Ibid.

16. Dan R. Crawford, *The Wedgewood Baptist Shootings: Night of Tragedy, Dawning of Light* (Colorado Springs, Colo.: Shaw Publishers, 2000), p. 69.

CHAPTER 12

HOSTAGE SITUATIONS

> All at once, a sudden burst of gunfire directly behind him wrenched at his gut.
>
> For one unbelievably long movement there was a stunned stillness.
>
> People turned around in the pews in an attempt to comprehend what they had just heard...Then pandemonium broke out! Some people jumped to their feet and started rushing toward the aisles.
>
> Another burst of gunfire, this time to the left of the sanctuary, froze everyone in their tracks.
>
> "Sit down, please," Akmed ordered. "If you remain in your seats you will not be hurt. Do not worry. You will all be released." —from the Christian novel *September Strike* by Ward Tanneberg.

The above scenario is taken from *September Strike,* but all examples of hostage situations are not the powerful words of fiction. They are the reality of life. In the First Baptist Church of Biloxi, Mississippi, located near the scenic Gulf Coast, an armed intruder took over the televised services on Sunday, April 14, 1977.

Pastor Frank Gunn had just begun preaching to a packed auditorium on the fact that no one knows how long they have left to live. Referring to a recent airplane crash, he asked the congregation, "What would you do if you had only several minutes to live?" It was at this moment that an emotionally disturbed retired Air Force major brought a German Shepherd and a gun into the sanctuary. An usher attempted to prevent him from coming in with the dog. The major pulled a pistol and in a struggle, the gun was discharged.

The major then walked to the platform, turned to the choir, and told them he wasn't going to hurt anyone. He shot the dog and then himself. Because of the sermon topic, many worshipers thought this scene was staged. Some even laughed, until they realized that the event was real. The denial response is not unusual. The major's wife said her husband had a history of emotional instability and believed that he was Jesus Christ.

While this event lasted approximately three minutes, many robberies and takeovers by the emotionally ill, the political zealot, or the spiritually irreverent last for much longer periods of time. Should this ever occur at your facility, you should know how to respond. Most importantly, perhaps, you should know what NOT to do. The emotional stressors are tenuous as victims are controlled inside your building, especially when the police show up outside, curtailing entrance and egress.

In Bowling Green, Kentucky, a man with two loaded guns interrupted a church service in September 1994.[1] A church member notified police at 11:45 a.m. that a person with two guns was in the balcony of the Glendale Baptist Church. By the time the officers arrived, a church member had already talked the man into giving up his guns, a .22 caliber rifle and a shotgun. The intruder, a former church member, was arrested and charged with first-degree wanton endangerment.[2]

Even the Grand Mosque at Mecca was taken over temporarily by gun-wielding fundamentalist Shia Islamics in 1979,[3] as they wanted to bring in a new millennium (by the Islamic calendar). Religious police and secular police who follow Islam assaulted the mosque and killed those responsible for the takeover.

A Strange Crime

Police call the "barricade hostage situation" one of the strangest of all crimes. There are many dynamics and several predictable stages. Used by terrorists a decade or two ago, it is now often used by criminals who are caught inside stores, banks, and other businesses while committing crimes. They hold other peoples lives in their hands with weapons and occasionally explosives.

Group hostage taking is difficult to comprehend. Hostage situations usually occur when the criminal is attempting another crime such as robbery or rape. The criminal is left to take a witness when he is surprised by the authorities or when he concludes that he cannot escape without a hostage.

When robbers take control of a sanctuary or congregational hall, the safety and control problems are the same, but group hostage-takers usually have an entirely unique agenda. When considering your options you should first remember how easy it is to kill. If a hostage-taker wanted death, he or she could easily use a 17-cent bullet. Shooting a rifle from a great distance is a low-risk crime. Coming in contact with the victim(s) is a high-risk crime. The hostage taker(s) have an agenda and a purpose for living hostages. Dead hostages are of little utility and almost always cause the police department hostage rescue team to respond with force. To this degree the hostages and the hostage-taker have a similar goal—that the hostages stay alive.

When an attack occurs, all precipitous, over-reactive, and violent behavior should be avoided. If anyone loses his cool, some of your members may be killed! We encourage congregations to plan for the possibility of a hostage takeover, so that your members will know how to cooperate in a response designed to decrease the loss of life and the dangers of spiraling violence.

What to Expect If a Group Hostage Attack Occurs

Violence is to be expected at the beginning. Gunfire, perhaps even the detonation of an explosive is designed to shock the group into submission. Profanity, threats of death, and further violence are all normal modes of operation in this form of crime. The criminals must use gunfire, violence, and profanity to decrease the likelihood of resistance and increase the likelihood of group submission. These criminals must obtain submission, otherwise the greater numbers of the congregation may subdue them. But be advised that while these offenders may not want to kill, they will if stressed or threatened.

To increase the level of safety, your leadership should stay calm and focused, urging the congregation to cooperate for the safety of the entire group. The scripture used to train missionaries being robbed or taken hostage is Psalms 141:3, "Set a watch, O Lord, before my mouth; keep the door of my lips."[4] This is sound advice. It is also normally sound advice to remain compliant. Those members of the congregation who resist or are non-compliant are at grave risk. Hostage takers often take a scapegoat to "show" they are serious about their intentions. Usually the scapegoat is the person who has given them the most difficulty during the earlier stages of the abductions.[5] It is called the "get rid of the JERK syndrome."

How to Respond to a Group Hostage Event

Do exactly what you are instructed to do. If the hostage-taker talks to you, let him know of your intent to comply. The words NO and NEVER can get you killed. These guys aren't likely to ask you to deny your faith, but otherwise they want control and compliance. By acquiescing, you give them what they want (control) and what you want (to keep on living). By acquiescing, you can become a "successful victim" and the congregation can be successful as well. Successful victims survive and usually don't even go to the hospital. Back in the days of an American skyjacking, the passengers had a 98 percent chance of survival in a negotiation,[6] but at best only an 87 to 88 percent chance of survival if the SWAT team was forced to come in.[7] In some developing nations, the survival chances decrease even more significantly.

Secondly, it is important to consider concessions, negotiation, attrition, or an amicable settlement. If the hostage-taker is willing to talk, perhaps there is someone in the congregation who can communicate. If you can "talk" him down, you will probably survive. If you maintain your composure and mental health, you will probably survive. Resistance should *never be offered in the face of overwhelming force.* Keep in mind that some of your members are police or security professionals. Many police departments require their officers to carry pistols at all times. Always remember that officers are trained not to use their weapons except to save a life. However, if there is a single hostage taker and the risks are high, they may feel forced to intervene. In the face of overwhelming force, they will (wisely) leave their pistols in their holsters. They have a responsibility for the groups' safety, not just for the safety of themselves and their family. In most hostage situations the hostage-taker does not resort to gunplay unless he feels threatened or that he is losing control.

Dos and Don'ts

- Do exactly what the gun holders demand.
- Don't do anything you are not ordered to do.
- Do not even speak unless ordered to, much less argue or debate with the hostage-taker.
- Once control has been established, a pastor or other church leader may ask for permission for a public prayer or a statement to remain calm. This will probably be allowed, because it is also to the hostage-taker's advantage.

One of the most effective ways to deter hostage situations is to have CCTV cameras or to have someone outside the sanctuary (perhaps in a sound booth or infant nursing station), observing the services. Usually, there will be a telephone in this room. If an intruder enters the service, the observer may alert the police.

Also, if there is a way to escape without being noticed, do so. Choir lofts, adjacent rooms, soundbooths, and infant nursing stations may offer this option. Make sure that your escape will not be detected. If you are uncertain, you are probably safer if you do not draw any attention to yourself. A quiet, undetected room could be the safest place around. If the room can be locked, lock it.

Remaining attentive and calm is very important. Remember that the hostage events usually do not last very long. The stateside hostage-taker usually wants to exit as soon as possible and avoid arrest. Sometimes it is to your benefit to provide what he requests, rather than accept the risk of violence. If he wants your offering so he can get out of town, give it to him. Money is a small price to pay for the safety of your congregation. A hostage-taker doesn't usually murder, but he may resort to killing if he is angered. Sometimes the hostage-taker simply wants attention from the media or the police and has no intention of harming anyone. However, this is something you usually do not know at the time the attack is occurring. Therefore, you need to remain calm and comply with his requests.

Endnotes

1. Associated Press, "Man With Gun Interrupts Worship, Then Surrenders," *Louisville* (Ky.) *Courier Journal,* 5 September, 1994, n.p.

2. Ibid.

3. Paul Wilkinson and Alasdaire M. Stewart, *Contemporary Research on Terrorism* (Aberdeen, United Kingdom: The University Press, 1987), p. 77.

4. Ps.141:3, Authorized (King James) Version.

5. Mayer Nudell and Norman Antokol, *No One a Neutral; Political Hostage-Taking in the Modern World* (Medina, Ohio: Alpha Publications, 1990), as found in *Security Management,* volume 34, no. 7, July 1990, p. 57-66.

6. Gail Bass, et al., (with the assistance of Joyce Peterson,) *Options for U.S. Policy on Terrorism* (Santa Monica, Ca.: The Rand Corporation [R-2764-RC], July 1981), p. 4.

7. Brian Jenkins, Janera Johnson, and David Ronfelt, *Numbered Lives: Some Statistical Observations From 77 International Hostage Episodes* (Santa Monica, Ca.: The Rand Corporation, [P-5905], July 1977), p. 27.

CHAPTER 13

CHILDREN AND YOUTH: SPECIAL RISKS

In Ventura, California, a drug-influenced dad decided to visit a church where visitors are welcomed and encouraged to attend worship services. This dad had plotted a crime and decided that the church provided the perfect opportunity. He wanted to abduct his son from the church nursery. A court order had barred him from seeing his child or his ex-wife, but he knew where they attended church every Sunday morning. The dad decided that he was going to gain permanent custody by abducting his child and fleeing the state.

Cruising the parking lot, he found his ex-wife's car and decided to carry out his plan. There was a problem, however. He was not aware that the church had implemented a "child numbering system." When a child is left at the nursery, the parent is given a number and a duplicate number is pinned to the child's clothing. When the service is over and the parent returns for his or her child, they must provide the matching number. Otherwise, the child is not released. The unsuspecting dad was unaware of this security feature. After observing the process, he decided to force his way into the class where he grabbed his son and fled.

The screams of children and adult attendants prevented the abduction. A husband and wife police team, Bob and Lynn Klamser, were entering the educational complex as the dad was exiting with his son. The nursery attendants were trailing, yelling for him to stop. The officers prevented the parental abduction with physical force and a takedown. Bob told co-author Quarles, "Chester, it's the only time I've ever had to fight at church."

Timing was crucial in this case. The church member/police officers were in the right place at the right time. Obviously a crime occurred, but a tort (a civil action) occurred as well. There are several questions that need to be answered about the procedures at your facility. Do your children or youth leaders receive any training? What are your policies and procedures? If this dad had been successful, what are the legal responsibilities of your religious organization? Would litigation be successful in this case? How else might this crime have been prevented?

Child Abuse

In Bullitt County, Kentucky, a 46-year-old woman was summoned to appear in Bullitt District Court to face charges accusing her of fondling and assaulting two girls during Sunday school classes.[1] She was accused of touching the girls in the genital area, pinching their eyebrows, punching them in the stomach, and dunking their heads in a toilet. This case came to the public's attention when two sets of parents filed a criminal complaint based on stories from their four-and-five-year-old girls. Both parents allege that the girls were threatened with harm if they told anyone.

This information was brought to the attention of the pastor, who immediately told the teacher that she was under investigation and could not attend services until the matter was settled. He also encouraged the parents to alert authorities. Then, a third family came forward with similar allegations. The pastor talked with some 35 families whose children may have come into contact with this teacher, but no other allegations were made. The pastor said, "We do background checks through the court system. We have good policies and procedures. I don't know what more we could do."[2]

The accused pleaded innocent to the charges after being indicted on two counts of first-degree sexual abuse, two counts of terroristic threatening, and two counts of fourth-degree assault. She was released on her own recognizance on the condition that she was to have no contact with anyone under the age of 16 without supervision, including in church and school, and she was required to undergo a psychological evaluation. The trial is still pending. Her lawyer called her "a truly God fearing woman," and said that it had been difficult for her to be away from her church. She now attends another church.[3]

According to the pastor, their congregational policy manual requires that two workers take children to the restroom. When he was notified that this woman had taken children in alone, he had immediately removed her from this position. His quick action may have prevented other children from being abused and may have prevented these two children from enduring additional abuse.[4]

Child Molestation

In Tennessee, a pastor was approached by a church member who made an accusation against a deacon youth leader. The deacon was accused of making inappropriate remarks and of "fondling" a teenage girl, another church member's teenage daughter.[5] As the youth leader, this deacon often provided transportation. However, he established an environment in which he could easily commit his crime. After letting his daughter off at their home, "so she could study," he made inappropriate remarks and fondled the teenage girl as he was taking her home.

The pastor discussed these accounts with the deacon privately. He denied the incident. It was the teenager's word against his.[6] The deacon claimed "the girl had a mental problem and was trying to sabotage his ongoing youth ministry." However, the girl's mother began to discuss the incident with other mothers, and very quickly it was discovered that her daughter was not the first who had been touched or who had been talked to inappropriately. Other parents came forward and told of similar incidents. Some female members in their twenties and thirties alleged inappropriate behavior even 10 to 20 years before—establishing a pattern of behavior over a long period. He is alleged to have hugged, touched, and kissed several young teenagers. His "touching" included cupping breasts and buttocks.

How could this situation have been avoided? How must it be resolved? It placed the pastor and the church in a very vulnerable situation. The deacon was alleged to have victimized several young girls over an extended period of time. Yet, prior to this event, he had an excellent personal reputation and was a charter member of the church. Some members believed in his innocence while others believed him to be guilty. While the pastor and the deacons were desperately attempting to reconcile the issue, several families chose to leave the church. This tragedy had a dramatic effect on the church in a very short time period.

The investigation uncovered the fact that similar complaints had been made to two former pastors. One pastor didn't do anything and ignored the complaint. The second pastor asked the deacon to resign, but backed down when he saw tertiary problems developing over the issue. It was some years later, when a third pastor heard fresh complaints that action was finally taken. As the aberrant deacon's life spun out of control, he made new and inappropriate telephone calls to other women of the church. Some were tape-recorded. He also wrote inappropriate letters to other women and girls. These letters and recordings were shared among the women of the church and the incidents were discussed with others. The pastor approached the deacon and the church offered to fund professional counseling and to seek reconciliation with the church at some point in the future. The deacon's only reaction, however, was hostility and absolute denial.

The pastor had to make a decision so he decided, with the blessing of the deacons, to have a church trial and to present the evidence to the church-at-large in a business meeting. The purpose of the meeting was previously announced, under the guidelines of 1 Corinthians: 5, as well as other scriptures relating to church discipline. The hearing was held and the deacon again denied any wrongdoing and refused to consider counseling or stepping down from his youth leadership role. Based on the testimony of numerous victims, both adult and youth, the church decided to rescind the deacon's ordination and he was barred from the fellowship of this church. During this time frame, he was also discharged from his secular job for sexual harassment in non-church related incidents.

The debarred deacon is now the Sunday school director and a deacon in another church in another city! The new pastor called the former church when he questioned the unusual manner in which he affiliated himself with the new church. The pastor was fully informed as to the particulars by church staff members, but chose to accept the former deacon's version of these events. Even though the new pastor had full knowledge of the former church's position, he still allowed the appointment of this man to high office almost immediately in his church. Today, the molester supervises the youth program in his present church.[7]

Would a court determine that the first two pastors were liable? Probably. Would a court determine that the church was negligent in appointing or continuing to appoint this man? Probably. Should the parents have filed charges with the local police? Absolutely. Was the church policy deficient by allowing the molester the opportunity to transport teenagers alone? Certainly. Would it be helpful if that church (and yours) had a policy requiring two adults be present when transporting children and youths? Certainly. If another molestation occurs at the new church, will the pastor and the congregation be liable? Certainly.

A case in point: In Richmond, Kentucky, a church pastor was arrested and accused of acting irresponsibly by allowing a suspected child abuser to work at the church day-care center. The pastor was charged with criminal facilitation of first-degree sexual abuse and third-degree criminal abuse.[8] The state had already revoked the day-care center's license several months prior to the arrest. The administrative judge's ruling hinted that the state was aware, as early as 1995, that there was a problem with the accused person's alleged contact with children at this center. A judgment required the accused to be supervised during any contact with the day-care children. In 1988, the police recommended that the pastor enforce the ruling, and that this person be barred from contact with children.

Nevertheless, as late as March 1999, the accused transported children on a bus without an adult monitor. The accused employee was indicted on 12 felony counts, nine counts of first-degree sexual abuse, two counts of first-degree sodomy, and one count of first-degree rape. Records revealed that the accused had been charged previously with six counts of first-degree sexual abuse.[9] Is the pastor liable? Absolutely. Will the parents of the victims win a large settlement against this church? In all probability.

In February 2001, the pastor pled guilty to misdemeanor "facilitation of menacing" and was given a $250 fine.[10] The assistant district attorney felt that this was the best way to settle the case and get a conviction. In September 2001, a jury convicted the day care director of one felony charge of sexually abusing a young boy, and four misdemeanor charges of non-sexual abuse. He was sentenced to five years in prison but is free on bond while he appeals.[11]

Another worker was sentenced to 120 days in jail after she was found guilty of nonsexual abuse of children at the same center. While this event may be over for the workers, it is not over for the children. There will be emotional trauma from these events and the parents have the option of suing the pastor and the church in civil court.

How would your congregation handle accusations against the deacon or the day-care employee? How would your pastor, priest, or rabbi handle the situation? Would an investigation be conducted in a fair and consistent manner when serious charges are made? Would the membership trust the decision of the leadership or would it splinter the congregation? When it comes to protecting our children and our youth, we must have procedures in place to ensure that they are not being victimized in any way and that they are safe and secure while in our midst.

Sexual Abuse

In Portland, Oregon, the Roman Catholic Church apologized for one of the nations' largest cases of sexual abuse by a priest and agreed to pay an undisclosed sum to 22 men, most of them former altar boys, who said they had been molested as far back as 50 years ago. The men accused the priest of enticing them to engage in sexual acts from 1950 until 1974.[12] The accused had served at a home for troubled and abused boys, as well as in parish churches. The 22 men came forward after a man filed suit in Seaside, Oregon, in 1999. The church agreed to develop a task force to recommend policies for avoiding abuse, as well as to review the files of active priests who had been subjects of complaints and to offer counseling to other victims.

The civil suit alleged that the archbishop had failed to notify the parishioners of the priest's past, that he had failed to monitor him, and he had failed to advise authorities and other adults that he should be accompanied during youth activities. They could not press criminal charges because the statute of limitations had expired; however, the plaintiffs filed a lawsuit for $44 million in damages.[13]

In 1998, the Catholic Diocese in Dallas, Texas, agreed to pay more than $30 million to 11 former altar boys who said a former priest had molested them. The priest was sentenced to life in prison.[14] Archbishop Michael Sheehan of Santa Fe once estimated the cost of settling sexual-abuse lawsuits at $50 million. The archdiocese settled 45 suits against a former priest, but the amounts were kept confidential. The nation's largest known priest abuse case (in terms of the number of individuals claiming to have been abused) occurred in Massachusetts and involved a priest accused by 99 people of molesting them in the 1950s and 1960s. He pleaded guilty in 1993 to 28 of these charges, and was sentenced to 18 to 20 years in prison.[15]

The Archdiocese of Chicago spent $2.8 million on sexual misconduct cases in 1993, the same year it ran a nearly $4.5 million deficit. As the issue of clergy sexual abuse continues to become public, additional lawsuits are expected. In 1994, the National Conference of Catholic Bishops voted for changes in church law to make it easier to dismiss abusive clergy from the priesthood, as well as appointing independent review boards to handle allegations.[16]

In Louisa, Kentucky, an elderly Baptist preacher was convicted of sexually abusing boys from his congregation.[17] The pastor was convicted in 1996 and is serving a 25-year sentence in a nursing facility at the Kentucky State Reformatory in LaGrange, Kentucky. He was charged with inviting boys to spend nights on his farm, where he would use a gorilla costume and a coffin to frighten the boys into his bed. Eight victims came forward to testify that he had fondled them. His attorney asked Governor Paul Patton of Kentucky to pardon him, claiming that as an 83-year-old man, he is harmless. The state attorney general's office opposed the request.

In Dover, New Hampshire, a 28-year-old Rochester school district employee was arrested for sexually assaulting two boys, aged 13 and nine. He had befriended the boys through the Mormon Church in Sommersworth and through the Boy Scouts. After his arrest, it was discovered that he was wanted in Kentucky on similar charges.[18]

In Petersburg, Virginia, a pastor was convicted of 15 sexual crimes spanning his long career as a religious and political leader. The jury recommended 161 years in prison.[19] He was originally indicted on 39 felony charges ranging from rape to aggravated sexual battery, all involving girls. However, five charges were added and 14 were dropped because of the prosecutions problems in fixing dates to the allegations. At the trial, the five accusers, ages 13, 14, 16, 18, and 25 described their victimization in graphic detail. The pastor took advantage of the girls he was supposed to counsel. He often charmed the families by providing food, money, and medicine.[20]

Pornography and Pedophiles

The pastor was proud of his family. His youngest was a vivacious and attractive 11-year-old girl. She radiated the positive environment of her family, and all eyes would travel to this sweet girl. It was this beauty that attracted a predator within their church, a pedophile who, based on predivorce allegations, was also guilty of incest.

The predator was a professional photographer, highly skilled with cameras, lights, and backdrops.[21] Employed as a public agency photographer, he worked after hours at weddings and contracted for portrait work. His specialty was children. Attracted to the beauty of the pastor's daughter, he began visiting the pastor's family. It was during these visits that he first offered to photograph the little girl, making a full portfolio as a gift for the pastor's family. At first the pastor was appreciative, but then he began to feel apprehensive about the way this guy looked at his little girl. The pastor didn't know why, but he felt uncomfortable with this guy's interest in his daughter.

Over a period of time, the photographer occasionally came by the pastoral residence when the pastor was not at home. Then one day he came by when the children were alone for a few minutes. It was at this time the pastor told his church member to *never, ever* come again unless or until he was personally invited by the pastor. All future portfolio plans were cancelled at that time.

It was only later, when the pastor counseled the photographer's wife during the separation and divorce period that he began to realize that this church member wasn't normal insofar as his relationships and attraction to children. The pastor thanks God for giving him the intellect needed to interpret the photographer's bizarre behavior. Another pervert was thwarted in his deviancies.

Investigations of Religious Leaders

As a state police investigator, co-author Quarles was occasionally asked to investigate members of the clergy and lay members of the religious community. The son of a pastor who later served as a state denominational administrator, he knew how to deal with members of the religious community, both clergy and laity. It was in this capacity that he worked statutory rape cases involving males and females, as well as adult rape charges of the clergy. Some of these charges were substantiated during the investigation and resulted in indictments and criminal prosecutions. Others were unconfirmed.

Regardless of the outcome, each investigation and case had an impact on the congregation. Each congregation was shaken and fellowship disrupted as members took sides and as lines were drawn. It is difficult to accept a verdict of guilt or innocence when you are closely involved with the victim or with the accused. Some members will always believe that charges are "trumped up," mistaken, or erroneous.

Co-author Quarles has interviewed both males and females of all ages, who have been raped, fondled, groped, and abused by religious leaders, religious institutions' staff members, and volunteers. As demonstrated by the accounts listed on the previous pages, these events cause great harm to the congregation, the community, and the victim.

Child Molestation and Exploitation

This crime has lifetime consequences, both immediately and throughout the victim's lifetime. The National Center of Child Abuse discloses that in 89 percent of all sexual assaults, seduction, and exploitation, the children are abused by someone they know. This Federally funded center also reports that one out of every five girls and one out of eight boys is a victim of some form of sexual abuse by age 12. Kenneth Wooden, in his book *Child Lures,* wrote that as many as 20 percent of all girls and seven percent of boys will experience some kind of sexual abuse by age 18.[22] Gavin De Becker, author of *Protecting the Gift,* wrote that one in three girls and one in six boys will have sexual contact with an adult.[23]

The impact of sexual abuse on the child is severe, the trauma of the event lasting through the victim's lifetime. Many studies conclude that the molestation increases the likelihood of youth and adult alcohol consumption, drug abuse, and even the counterphobic indicators of promiscuity.

First, we must accept the fact that we cannot identify a child molester or a pedophile by appearance. There are no visible indicators guaranteeing recognition of pedophiles. Pedophiles do not necessarily have beady eyes and long, skinny noses. They don't wear black hats and sinister expressions. They are usually men, often distinguished men (most sexual predators are men),[24] and often these men are well-known leaders. (A Church Mutual Insurance Company brochure states that 90 percent of all sexual predators are men).[25] While over 50 percent of all child sexual abuse is incestuous in nature,[26] the rest is not. The Church Mutual Insurance Company says that, "all too often, it is a person in a position of trust and frequent contact with children—such as a teacher, child care worker, camp counselor, youth minister, or even a clergy person."[27]

Under any circumstances, 90 percent of all sexual abuse is committed by someone the child knows—not by a stranger.[28] Many child molesters are married with children, violating the mythical stereotype that the average American has of these deviants. One of co-author Quarles' first criminal investigations into child molestation involved a married pastor with children and grandchildren.

The pastor/molester would visit single parent families and develop relationships with their children, particularly in this case, the boys. It was easy for the perpetrator to develop relationships with the boys because they were starved for mature male companionship. Their fathers were absent. The pastor took the boys camping, fishing, and hunting. After establishing trust relationships, he took advantage of their youth and their innocence, leaving them with emotional scars which would be difficult to heal, as well as negative memories associated with "church activities." The case was brought to light after the youth began having nightmares and emotional problems. When the matter was discussed within the church family, other victims came forward.

> **The Most Dangerous Ages for a Child**
>
> - Boy's danger age is 9 to 11.
> - Girl's danger age is 11 to 14.
> - The 14-year-old girl is at the peak of her risk. If she avoids rape by the age of 16, her risk rate of 25 percent (or 1 reported rape to every 4 females) will be decreased significantly over her lifetime.

We must be on guard with individuals who want to spend time with our children alone, and strive to develop close, personal relationships. It is through these relationships that the molester or pedophile becomes successful. A pedophile often befriends a single female parent and offers to help with her children. Or they develop a close relationship with a child through coaching or teaching.

Most child molesters are bisexual. In a true pedophile versus homosexual relationship, the sex of the child is not important; however, the age and immaturity of the child is extremely important. The molester wants a child or a young person regardless of the sex. The traditional descriptions of homosexuality or heterosexuality don't exist for the pedophile. Pedophiles seek children because of the innocence of their youth, that they are untouched by others, and that they feel they can influence them.

Ways to Reduce Victimization

Develop policies and procedures for all activities. For example, two adult workers must accompany all children and youths during all events. Also, enforce the policy that you are required by law to report incidents of criminal activity unless those crimes were discovered in legally protected counseling sessions (licensed psychologist, psychiatrist, or clergy). Otherwise, you will be concealing a crime. "Misprison" is the name of the crime for concealing a lesser crime, otherwise known as a misdemeanor. In most states you can go to jail for up to one year on a misdemeanor.

A serious crime is known as a felony. Felons are sentenced to prison for more than one year. When you conceal a felony, the charge is called obstruction of justice, and the concealment of a felony is a felony. In other words, you can go to prison for not reporting a serious crime. Hiding crime and molestation, deceiving others, or camouflaging crimes is a serious matter–and often a crime itself. Keep in mind, too, that even if you have not committed a crime, that you may be found negligent in a civil court hearing for failing to provide a safe environment and by not having and enforcing policies, procedures, and systems to protect children.

Youth leaders should be encouraged not to object to the presence of other adults. One key point of molestation avoidance is to remember that employees or volunteer workers should not direct any of the youth activities alone. Other mature adults should be present. Be leery if activities are private and parents aren't invited to attend. If parents and other adults are not included, it may be an indication that the church worker has something to hide. **Be suspicious of any person who wants to spend time alone with children and would prefer that other adults not be there.** Remember: Secrecy helps the molester thrive. Openness prevents sexual abuse and exploitation.

Also be suspicious of any person whose home is where neighborhood children like to congregate. Molesters make their homes into a child-friendly atmosphere by offering cookies, soft drinks, and ice cream. As the children get older, alcohol and drugs may also be provided. **Molesters and exploiters always have time for children.**

Being Proactive

By being proactive, both in policy and in standard operating procedures involving all children and youth activity, you can protect your congregation's youth, as well as shield yourself from the risks of litigation. The Church Mutual Insurance Company emphasizes this point in their policy material:

> You are the guardian of the spiritual well being of your church's children and teens. When they are in your care—whether on or off church property—you also are a guardian of their physical and often emotional, well being. This is not only a moral duty; in many cases it is your legal responsibility. As your youth ministry grows, so does your exposure to legal risk resulting from personal injury.

> By safeguarding your congregation's youth, you will take the important first step in protecting their well being—and shield your church from

the considerable financial and emotional disruption that inevitably results when injury, damages, and lawsuits occur.[29]

Technology Can Protect Reputations

Closed Circuit Television (CCTV) is a worthwhile investment, especially in the nursery, day care center, kindergarten, and in your school. Used in almost every bank, grocery store, and shopping center in America, a CCTV could be a tremendous benefit as it documents and records all activities within reach of the camera lens. Indoor CCTV units are fairly inexpensive to purchase and maintain. Indoor units are self-contained while the outside units require canopy, windshield wipers, dehumidifiers, heaters, and air conditioners. Outdoor units are very expensive.

Cameras should be installed at prominent locations overlooking primary child care areas, baby beds, educational, and recreation areas. Used with a timer, the date and time are recorded on the film's surface, and it may be possible to deduce whether possible improper or criminal conduct took place out of the range of the camera's eye.

Other Precautionary Practices

Child care areas should also have sign-in and sign-out sheets that are maintained in administrative files for at least two years. Daily schedules and sick slips should also be maintained on both employees and children. These records prove who was present at a particular time and can often document or disprove a particular event. These records have demonstrated that misrepresentations also occurred in some cases.

Child care workers should also be given an exceptional pre-employment background investigation, even if congregation members are working in these slots. On the application, obtain each job applicant's permission to investigate criminal records, credit records, apartment and housing records, and employment histories. You will be glad you did.

Co-author Quarles has performed hundreds of background investigations over a period of years for a publicly funded, Federally supported boarding trade school. Pedophiles, drug dealers, and prostitutes applied for employment there with relative frequency. It was his job to filter them out through background scrutiny. These people are attracted to employment in places where crime targets are young, impressionable, easily intimidated, or frightened.

| **Remember to Do the Following:** | **Summary**

This chapter is not all-inclusive. While religious organizations are not always required to comply with state mandates governing child care facilities, you should carefully review the state guidelines to ensure that you are reasonably in compliance with state mandated security guidelines. Being in compliance will help protect your children, keep you out of court, and your religious organization out of the news. |
| :--- | :--- |

Remember to Do the Following:

- Develop policies and procedures for all activities.
- Screen all volunteers and employees with a background check the applicant has agreed to.
- Check with former pastors, priests, rabbis, and staff employees of their congregation.
- Consider the use of CCTV systems.

Endnotes

1. Jason Riley, "Teacher Abused 2 Girls, Say Parents," *Louisville* (Ky.) *Courier Journal*, 8 July, 2000, n.p.

2. Ibid.

3. Tonia Holbrook, "Woman Pleads Innocent to Abuse," *Louisville* (Ky.) *Courier Journal*, 12 December 2000, n.p.

4. Jason Riley, "Teacher Abused 2 Girls, Say Parents," *Louisville* (Ky.) *Courier Journal*, 8 July 2000, n.p.

5. A pastor who wishes to remain anonymous. Private interview by Chester L. Quarles, January 1998.

6. The statement of the accused youth leader, whose personal identity and church identity will remain confidential.

7. From a confidential source, December 2000.

8. Associated Press, "Pastor, Former Employee of Church Day Care Arrested," *Louisville* (Ky.) *Courier Journal*, May, 1999, n.p.

9. Ibid.

10. Associated Press, "Former Day-Care Operator Makes Deal, Avoids Jail." *Louisville* (Ky.) *Courier Journal*, February 2001, n.p.

11. Ibid.

12. Associated Press, "Catholic Church to Pay 22 Men Who Said Priest Molested Them," *Louisville* (Ky.) *Courier Journal*, 11 October, 2000, p. A9.

13. Ibid.

14. Ibid.

15. Ibid.

16. David Briggs. "Sex Abuse Scandals Likely to Cost Catholic Church Millions," *Louisville* (Ky.) *Courier Journal*, 23 January, 1994, p. 13-A.

17. Roger Alford, Associated Press, "Patton Is Asked to Pardon Jailed Sex Offender, 83," *Louisville* (Ky.) *Courier Journal,* 17 November 2000, n.p.

18. Associated Press, "Sex-Crime Suspect Being Held in New Hampshire," *Louisville* (Ky.) *Courier Journal*, 27 November, 1999, p. 7-B.

19. Bill Geroux, "Petersburg Church," *Richmond* (Va.) *Times Dispatch*, 21 June, 1987, n.p.

20. Ibid.

21. A denominational leader in the southeastern United States. Private interview by Chester Quarles, October 1999

22. Kenneth Wooden, *Child Lures: What Every Parent and Child Should Know About Preventing Sexual Abuse and Abduction* (Arlington, Texas: The Summit Publishing Group, 1995), p. xi.

23. Gavin De Becker, *Protecting the Gift: Keeping Children and Teenagers Safe (and Parents Sane)* (New York: The Dial Press of Random House Publishers, 1999), p. 15.

24. Gavin De Becker. *Protecting the Gift: Keeping Children and Teenagers Safe (and Parents Sane)*: BDD Audio Tape Series, Random House Publishers, 1999). An audiotape.

25. The Church Mutual Insurance Company, "Safety Tips on a Sensitive Subject: Child Sexual Abuse": The Protection Series (Merrill, Wis.: The Church Mutual Insurance Company, 2000), p. 2.

26. Kenneth Wooden, *Child Lures: What Every Parent and Child Should Know About Preventing Sexual Abuse and Abduction* (Arlington, Tex.: The Summit Publishing Group, 1995) p. 3.

27. The Church Mutual Insurance Company, "Safety Tips on a Sensitive Subject: Child Sexual Abuse": The Protection Series (Merrill, Wis.: The Church Mutual Insurance Company, 2000), p. 2.

28. Gavin De Becker, *Protecting the Gift: Keeping Children and Teenagers Safe (and Parents Sane)* (New York: The Dial Press of Random House Publishers, 1999), p. 15.

29. The Church Mutual Insurance Company, "Youth Safety and Your Church: The Protection Series" (Merrill, Wis.: The Church Mutual Insurance Company, 1998), p. 1.

CHAPTER 14

Religious Leaders

Consider some of the big names of the religious world: Billy Graham, Pope John Paul II, the Dalai Lama, and Louis Farrakan. Have you recognized the "celebrity status" of these religious people? Perhaps this is not the best term, but each of these leaders meets the definition of a celebrity. They are well-known leaders who may or may not be liked because of their teachings.

Unfortunately, there are predators in our society who wish to harm religious leaders. The motive behind the need to harm them is difficult to discern. Why would someone want to shoot the Pope? Why would someone want to harm Billy Graham? What purpose would that serve? We can't always answer these questions, but we can provide you with examples of attempts against religious leaders.

Granted, we have individuals in our society who are in need of psychiatric treatment and counseling. This was well demonstrated in the assassination attempt on President Reagan. John Hinkley wanted to "demonstrate" his love for actress Jodie Foster. We shudder at the very concept of his intense feelings because we don't comprehend his reasoning, even though we understand it from a psychosocial approach.

We have studied cases where individuals have followed "celebrity" ministers from city to city, in an attempt to talk to them. Eventually they crossed the line and became stalkers. We have cases where females have followed ministers "on a mission from God" and wanted to "meet" with the minister. We have examples where rabbi's and priest's lives have been threatened.

When the media has an opportunity to damage a reputation or to shed some unfavorable light on a congregation, can we expect them to do so? Just how badly can one allegation damage a congregation? Are there activist groups wanting to destroy the reputation of particular religious leaders or limit the influence of specific congregations?

With the proliferation of "hate" groups who work against the Jewish and African-American communities and sometimes Islamic as well, we know that individuals of faith must exercise extreme caution. When conservative religious groups take initiatives against abortion or homosexuality, they can expect a response from the radicals of those agendas. If a church takes a stand on a controversial issue, the church can expect trouble. While we cannot predict the certainty of trouble, we would encourage you to assess your community and examine the risk factors.

If your leader has worked several years to build a successful ministry, what is the possibility that one false allegation could derail, if not destroy, his career? Recognizing this possibility, we encourage religious leaders to examine their lifestyle to ensure that they not become the victims of a diabolical plot to destroy their ministry.

We have several examples of religious leaders and staff members having been assaulted, robbed, and raped. In Philadelphia, Pennsylvania, several rectories and convents were burglarized while the priests and nuns were praying.[1] On one occasion the priest returned to find a man inside his third-floor bedroom, claiming that he had been told by an old parish priest to go into the building to talk to a Brother Daniel. Luckily, the intruder was escorted out, avoiding any major crime or the appearance of inappropriate conduct.[2]

When the Reverend Rafael Suazo is called from his Villa Coralina Parish for a late night emergency at the Catholic Church's AIDS hospice in Rio Piedras, he contacts the police for an escort to and from the medical center.[3] He has been robbed and assaulted in the past, and held at gunpoint there at his rectory. He also told the co-authors about other priests who were shot at, beaten, and robbed. He recalled how the Reverend Elisco Castano, pastor of Our Lady of Pilar Church in Rio Piedras, was murdered in the church rectory during an apparent robbery. Castano's brother had been bound and gagged during a previous robbery some four years before.

In one incident, a bullet grazed another priest during a church holdup. His rectory had been burglarized and robbed 13 times in the past eight years.[4] There are other reported cases involving couples who requested marital consultations, but when the priest opened the door, he was robbed after they pulled their guns.[5]

In December 1992, a rabbi was stabbed twice, just a few doors away from his synagogue. Police said that Rabbi Shaya Apter, aged 62, barely escaped with his life when his attacker tried to cut his throat. The rabbi fended off that blow, but his attacker stabbed him twice in the stomach before running away. Police labeled the attack as a bias attack or "hate" crime because he was attacked near a synagogue and was wearing a fur hat and other traditional Hasidic clothing.[6]

Pastors, rabbis, and other religious leaders are generally hesitant to accept personal security. Granted, there are many reasons for this including biblical principles, the fear of being labeled, the fear of being mocked, the fear that followers may question your belief, and more. We ask the question: "Is it necessary to have paid personal security?" In some cases, it is very necessary. When dealing with a large, influential congregation, it may be very necessary. The very survival and existence of the congregation often hinges on the leader and his or her followers. What is the threat to ministers?

We have reported cases where ministers have been robbed of their wallets and jewelry. We have reported cases where ministers have been assaulted with a baseball bat. We also encourage religious leaders to be careful of settings in which they could be entrapped, such as in situations where members of the opposite sex could make a move, then resort to blackmail.

What about cases in which the pastor, priest, or rabbi is threatened by members of the community or by individuals who are disheartened over a decision made by the congregational leadership? What are our responsibilities as congregational members to ensure that our leader is protected? Leaders who speak out about abortion, homosexuality, and other controversial topics are likely to be targeted. If someone who supports a gay lifestyle can bring discredit to the church leader, then he can discredit the congregation and reduce the effectiveness of the ministry. If the church is active in the community and reaching out to others, then it is a larger threat to those individuals advocating a different lifestyle. We encourage you to consider the role of your congregation and consider the consequences. If you believe that you must speak out, then you will need to exercise caution to keep from being a victim.

Pastors, priests, and rabbis also need security because they deal with people who are in very stressful situations. From death and disease to divorce, they are usually encountering emotional, as well as spiritual trauma. In previous chapters we shared the accounts of pastors who have been assaulted and even murdered while counseling couples going through divorce. Brother Roy Clark, a pastor at the Lake Harbor Baptist Church in the Ross Barnett Reservoir area outside of Jackson, Mississippi, was shot at close range by an angry husband.

Individuals protesting the church's moral position have threatened church leaders. For example, in Colorado, a church was vandalized with condoms and a blood-like substance in protest over the church's position on premarital sex. Members active in the gay rights movement have made frequent threats against pastors claiming that they are going to destroy the church. A minister in Louisville, Kentucky, resigned from his church after admitting to an extramarital affair. After the pastor left the state, it was rumored that the woman was planted by members of the gay rights movement who had openly made a vow to "get him out of town" because he was perceived as a "stumbling block" to accomplishing their radical agenda.

Reverend Roy Clark's Account

"It was just a regular day—the day I almost died. There was nothing different about it. I had just preached two revivals back-to-back on spiritual warfare. The last sermon before I was shot was on the Gadorene demoniac.

As a volunteer EMT, I was called at 4 a.m. about an abusive home situation and a possible injury. Driving to the location, I almost hit the lady, who happened to be one of my church members. She was running down the middle of the road. My wife and I gave her refuge in our home that night.

Her son, with a perfect attendance record, was to graduate with honors from our local high school the next week. The wife moved to a relative's home some distance away, so we volunteered to keep the son for the next week.

Shortly after being served papers by the deputies, her husband drove to my home. I met him at the door and stepped outside. He didn't seem angry or aggressive at all, but when I stepped out, he shot me.

I must share how grateful I am that God spared me. I was moments away from death, the doctor said. I could easily have died. There were many miracles that day. The EMTs and the air ambulance service responded quickly under poor weather circumstances, saving my life."[7]

Why should religious leaders be concerned about a threat? Because one false accusation could destroy their church and the ministry they have established. It is important that leaders are not confronted with protestors and that they avoid controversy. For example, if a leader attempts to have a conversation with opponents, it could easily escalate into a hostile confrontation. By editing film and sound tracks, the media could portray the institution and the leader in a negative light. A negative press could help further the goals of the opponents. Hecklers have been known to interrupt worship services. While your security personnel can handle this situation quickly, it creates a disturbance and can often provide negative coverage by the press.

A televangelist took on the "radical homosexual political action team" in one of his sermons. The radical homosexual rights activists in his community began harassing him and targeted him for continuing confrontation and several well-choreographed public incidents. The only public assault was a pie in his face. However, the attack was embarrassing and disruptive to the ministry. In addition to personal threats, facilities sometimes receive bomb threats and threats of arson.

We are not advocating that pastors, priests, or rabbis live in fear. However, we are advocating that religious leaders assess their vulnerability so that they can alter their lifestyle in appropriate ways. Additionally, we encourage "security awareness" and a more intense scrutiny of surroundings. This will help you avoid confrontations with hostile advocacy groups and to ensure that worship services are not interrupted with someone else's agenda.

Many congregations have added "security specialists" to their payrolls. There are many roles these individuals can play. For example, security officers can provide parking lot security to ensure that no one is breaking into the cars or that no one is loitering. They can watch over the classrooms to make sure that our young people are in the church service instead of getting into trouble. They can provide walking surveillance throughout the building and surveillance for the services. We encourage leaders to take precautions to avoid hostile confrontations, embarrassment, and any disruptive influence that might negatively influence their ministry.

The Problem

Many believers resist security applications at religious facilities and for congregational leaders. One of the biggest security obstacles is in the way believers interpret the understanding of sovereignty. Where does faith end and reason begin? "Isn't God responsible for my safety when I am in the center of his will?" worshipers may ask.

Security Suggestions

Pastors, rabbis, priests, and other religious leaders are generally hesitant to accept personal security. There is a fear of being labeled, the fear of being mocked, the fear that followers may question your beliefs and more. However, when considering the importance of your ministry and the need for you to continue as the leader, we advise you to proceed with great caution. Many religious leaders now use personal protection specialists to prevent embarrassment, frames, and attacks. You are the best judge of whether this will be appropriate for you and your institution and ministry.

Endnotes

1. Ralph Cipriano, "Now, Security at Churches Means Alarms, Razor Wire," *Philadelphia Inquirer*, 22 February, 1994, n.p.

2. Ibid.

3. Robert Friedman, "Island Criminals Lose Their Fear of God," *The San Juan* (Puerto Rico*) Star,* 8 September, 1991, n.p.

4. Ibid.

5. Ibid.

6. Tom Rafferty and Bob Kappstatter, "Knife Attack on Rabbi," *New York Daily Times,* 14 December, 1992, n.p.

7. Personal interview with Chester Quarles, December 1999.

CHAPTER 15

DISRUPTIVE INCIDENTS

Religious institutions are being targeted in many other ways. Sometimes picketers try to disrupt services, but usually they remain outside, across the street, or wave their signs of protest on thoroughfares and sidewalks. The picketing usually is targeted against churches or synagogues that have taken strong stands against specific politicized social concerns, such as gambling, homosexuality, birth control, or abortion. Usually these picketers are nonviolent, although occasionally tempers flare on both sides.

Usually these events can be expedited by the appropriate use of police and security services. The police normally maintain open roadways and the security personnel ensure that the uninvited don't intrude into institutional worship services. These disruptions are more likely to occur if you have a "famous" person attending or if a high-status guest speaker is giving the keynote address on that occasion. If the president or vice president of the United States is attending, you may well discover uniformed Secret Service officers guarding alternative doorways, ushering worshipers and guests in through metal detectors, and searching purses and briefcases where appropriate.

If a famous rabbi, a well-known evangelist, or the pope were visiting your worship center, you will normally find the order of events has been altered somewhat to ensure a safe and secure environment. Some of the enemies of these well known leaders may even be terrorists, capable of extreme violence, assassination, hostage taking, and even bombings. Bombings are the most often used terrorist strategy. Bombing or the threat of bombing is frequently used by those who wish to be disruptive.

Letter and Package Bombs

Bombs are frequently sent through the mail or courier services. This is very frightening. You open a box, or even a letter envelope, and it explodes, probably injuring hands, fingers, and eyes. The larger the bomb, the greater likelihood for extreme injury, incapacitation, and death. But even though a letter or package bomb is a surreptitious attack, there are several things that you can do. Some warnings can be found right there on the recipient address and the return address box.

Let's look at package bombs first. Your institution receives a package. You were not expecting any deliveries nor did you order anything. This is the first level of suspicion. Examine the package more thoroughly now. The U.S. Postal Service warning chart says that since bombers don't want to mail the explosive device at a post office where they might be identified, they put the postage on the box themselves. To ensure the package is sent, they usually put on too much postage. Now, there isn't anyone who can identify them. The Unabomber used this technique as well.[1] Excessive postage is a signal that something is wrong. The bomber also often puts on restrictive markings, such as PERSONAL, CONFIDENTIAL, FOR YOUR EYES ONLY (the recipient's). Many of these are packages are mailed at the highest postal rates, such as Air Mail or Special Delivery (the bomber doesn't want the explosive device to be handled over an exceptionally long period of time).

Package Bomb Warning Signals

- Sent Air Mail or Special Delivery.
- Marked "CONFIDENTIAL," "PERSONAL," "HANDLE WITH CARE," "RUSH," or "DO NOT DELAY."
- Excessive postage.
- Handwritten addresses.
- Titles, but no names.
- Incorrect titles.
- Misspellings of common words.
- Oily stains or discolorations.
- No return address.
- Excessive weight for packages normally received.

The bomber normally doesn't put a return address on the package or letter. If he does, it is probably fictitious. In fact, if your institution receives a questionable package, call the return address immediately. You may learn that this is a legitimate package. You may learn that there is no such "official" sender, leading you to question the package even more strongly.

Bombers rarely type out the address labels, but usually handprint them. Many of these are mismarked, mistitled, and common words are frequently misspelled. Also, many primitive explosives have liquids inside their core. Under contrasting heat and cold, humidity, and altitude problems the liquid may leak out onto the package surface. This is a very strong indicator the the package contains suspicious material.

Letter Bomb Warning Signals

- Rigid envelope.
- Lopsided or uneven envelope.
- Protruding wires or tinfoil.
- Excessive securing material such as cellophane or masking tape.
- Use of string on an envelope.
- Other visual distractions.
- Misspellings on common names and titles.
- Incorrect titles.

Sometimes the explosive material "leaks" onto the envelope itself. Frequently the bomber is afraid the device will explode before he mails it, so he uses masking tape, string, or excessive wrapping material to reduce this possibility. All in all, the letter bomb is "visually distracting." Look at what comes across your desk and at what you or your staff intends to open.

When letter bombs are sent, there are also noticeable PINS (pre incident indicators). These include an excessively rigid envelope, totally unlike a three or four page later. Because of the requirements for a detonator and the explosive compound itself, the letter may be lopsided or uneven. Sometimes wires or tinfoil protrudes. Protruding metals are a very strong indicator.

Institutional Bomb Threats

Telephoned bomb threats are an extremely common form of harassment against religious and ethnic institutions.[2] What do you do? More importantly, what do you *not* do. I am sure that they do not teach institutional bomb response techniques in divinity or rabbinical school. Your institutional security committee needs to obtain locally recommended response techniques from your local police, fire, and civil defense emergency response teams. However, perhaps we can give you a strong, positive start in your security planning and in the development of security policies.

The number one priority after a threat is to prevent panic. However, there is no way to predict if the threat is a prank, an irresponsible ruse to cover some other activity, a deliberate method of harassment designed to cause disruption or panic—or a serious warning of an impending explosion. Because of the potential risk of injury to persons, few threats can be ignored.

Most bomb threats are received by telephone, but a few are mailed, received through a courier service, or even faxed. If you ever receive such a threat, remain calm. Get control of your emotions before you start responding to the threat. Panic must be avoided. Follow your predetermined plan. In all probability you won't have a plan the first time the call comes in, but you will for subsequent threats.

History shows that bombing is by far the most common threat of terrorism and political disruption.[3] What if your worship center receives such a threat? Your risks are limited if only the pastor, priest, minister, or rabbi is present, along with a few staff members. But what if your facility is full at the time you receive the bomb threat? The caller may claim to represent an anti-Semitic organization or a local "action" group upset over your group's response to local abortion clinics. "You have been targeted," and the caller claims "a bomb was hidden in your complex last night." "It will detonate at noon today!" What do you do? What do you not do? These questions have already been asked in this section but they are very important. It is important to realize that there is little you could say to a bomber that would intensify or worsen the situation. Preparation is the key to reducing the damage that a bomb can do.[4]

A bomb threat is a very serious issue. The bad news is that over 50 percent of all terrorist attacks are in the form of bombings.[5] The good news is that most of the disruptions are in the forms of bomb threats, and then only two percent of all reported bomb threats turn out to be legitimate.[6] Overseas, embassies may have bomb detection equipment or explosive detection dogs. Many of these resources are available in Washington, D.C., and other metropolitan areas, but you may be hundreds of miles from this equipment or these dogs when you need them.

While a visual search of a bomb-threat area, is always a top priority, it is recognized that it is difficult to find plastic explosives and some of the new high-order explosive materials. A small bomb made of a hi-tech base can cause a lot of damage. Bomb detection equipment normally detects dynamite, TNT, firebombs, and other primitive explosives. These explosives emit a chemical vapor that is easily detectable by the equipment or by the dogs. The more modern plastics emit only a very slight vapor. Occasionally, neither dogs nor the standard equipment detects these vapors in small bombs.

Only well-trained federal, state, or local police bomb technicians have the skills and equipment needed to defuse or move explosive ordinance. The threat is too high for you and others in your midst. Evacuate all personnel to a safe area while calling the proper authorities. You may choose to make a "sweep" of the area, but remember that radio transmitters, light switches, and even flashlight beams set off some bombs.

The first step your institution should make in dealing with the threat of bombs is to develop an emergency evacuation plan. If you have a preexisting evacuation plan for either fire or natural disaster, it may also be appropriate, with minor modifications, for a bomb threat. By rehearsing the evacuation plan, at least among your institutional leaders, you can move expeditiously.

Those who want you to evacuate want the maximum disruption. They want panic and a spontaneous, chaotic, unplanned, nondirectional exit. They are denied this option when you evacuate in a well-planned and orderly manner. The risk is not over upon exiting, however. The bomb could be in your parking lot, while the telephoned threat is used as a method to get more people nearer to it. It would be best to evacuate away from parked vehicles until the authorities can check out this threat.

When a bomb threat has been received, there will always be a strong reaction to the call. Genuine or not, if handled improperly, you will create havoc. If the call is directed to a particular person or to an institution where there is a vacuum of leadership, or where there is no advanced planning to handle such threats with an organized approach, the chances are the call will result in panic—one of the most effective weapons used by terrorists and criminals alike.

Panic is one of the most contagious of all human emotions. Caused by fear—fear of the unknown or the known. Once a state of panic—the ultimate achievement for the caller—has been created, the potential for personal injury and property damage is dramatically increased.[7]

What should you do if you receive a threat by mail or a telephone call comes into your institutional offices? A harsh voice says, "A *bomb* has been placed in your building. It will be detonated precisely within an hour." The first tendency for the person answering the phone is to slam the phone down and run out of the office yelling that a bomb is in the building. But this is precisely what you should not do. Remember that no more than two percent of all threats are real[8] in even the most dangerous terrorism influenced countries.

There is no way of predicting whether a bomb threat will be a thoughtless prank, an irresponsible ruse, a deliberate method of harassment designed to cause disruption or panic—or a warning of an impending explosion. But because the potential risk of injury to persons is so high, few threats can be ignored.[9]

Bombs can be "intelligent," their fuses igniting from timers, height, pressure, temperature, garage door openers, burglar alarms, or even by a police radio transmission. If your institution gets a telephone threat, the first step is to follow the checklist we will provide. Think and avoid panic. While you will want to hang-up on the caller, you shouldn't because he or she can give you the information you need. Perhaps you can defuse the situation. It's unlikely that you can make the circumstances worse, after all the caller just threatened to harm you and the building you are in.

Many bomb threats are very precise. The caller usually says that the bomb is set to go off within a prescribed period. If this statement is a lie, then there's not much you can do to alter it. You probably don't have the skills necessary to stop the explosion, but the person answering the telephone can influence the situation immensely. The first step is to "listen" to the caller. You can learn a lot from what the caller says. Do you have caller ID? If you do, see if you can identify the number. If another staff member is present, get them to call the police on another line and give the basics of what you are experiencing now. If you have tape recording equipment available in your office, turn it on for the call. At the very least this taped record will increase your credibility for the police investigation. In some cases, the tape could lead to a resolution and the identity of the perpetrator.

Ask the bomb caller to reveal where the bomb was placed. Try to get the caller to reveal this information. Sometimes they will tell you, at other times, they will not, but if you don't ask you will never know. At the very least, this technique gives security teams a place to begin their search.[10] Sometimes you can determine if the bomb is a hoax. Ask them if the bomb is in a specific location, but name a site that doesn't exist. If the caller says the bomb is there, you know that it is not true. A safety sweep should be made. Searches should be completed, just to ensure this, but it is likely this is a "scare tactic" rather than a real bombing.

Sometimes ruses are used by the person receiving the call. The ruse can also be used to determine if someone knowledgeable about your schedule is making the threat. You could say something like this. "Oh, no! There's a bunch of school kids on a fieldtrip over here today." Ask the caller if he wants their deaths on his conscience.

Some spontaneous reactions have included these statements: "That's a lie. There is no bomb here. Nobody would want to bomb *this* facility!" This ploy will sometimes make the caller try to "prove' to you that he is serious, particularly if he wants a big bang, but not deaths and injuries.

Other telephone receptionists have hung up on the caller, preferably while he is speaking. You could say, as if to someone else in your office, "it's just another crazy kid calling in a false bomb threat." This may cause the bomb threat caller to call again and tell you where the risk is. This, of course, is in the case of a genuine threat.

Bomb Threat Call Checklist

Ask:
- **When** will it go off?
- **Where** is it located?
- **What** type of bomb is it?
- **What** type of explosive is it?
- **Why** are you doing this?
- **Who** are you?

See Anti-Defamation League, *Security for Community Institutions: A Handbook* (4th edition).

The Denver (Col.) Police Department "Bomb Threat Call Checklist" is a basic tool. It simply asks every basic question that a police officer or a news reporter would need in order to substantiate a probable event. This checklist is recorded in the Anti-Defamation League booklet, *Security for Community Institutions: A Handbook* (4th edition).

A Telephone Bomb Threat Checklist is a good tool. Give it to staff members and telephone volunteers. Distribute it throughout your organization.

Comprehensive Telephone Bomb Threat Checklist

❑ What TIME was the threat received?_____

❑ What LINE/NUMBER was called at your facility?_____

❑ WHEN will this bomb detonate?_____

❑ WHERE was the bomb placed?_____

❑ WHAT does the bomb look like?_____

❑ HOW MANY bombs were placed?_____

❑ WHY was the bomb placed there?_____

❑ WHO or WHAT GROUP planted the bomb?_____

❑ Was the threat caller MALE or FEMALE?_____

❑ Give the APPROXIMATE AGE of the caller._____

    ❑ Adult?_____ Teenager?_____ Child?_____

❑ EMOTIONAL STATE of the caller. _____

    ❑ Calm?_____ Excited?_____ Angry?_____

❑ Were there any BACKGROUND NOISES?_____

    ❑ ie.: Train?_____ Ships?_____ Airport?_____ Factory?_____ Traffic?_____

    _____ Marketplace?

❑ Did you detect any ACCENT?_____

❑ What was the probable NATIONALITY of the caller?_____

❑ What was the probable ETHNIC BACKGROUND of the caller?_____

❑ What was the RATE OF SPEECH of the caller?_____

    ❑ Slow?_____ Normal?_____ Rapid?_____ Excited?_____

❑ What was the VOLUME OF THE SPEAKER?_____

    ❑ Soft?_____ Normal?_____ Loud?_____

❑ What was the VOICE QUALITY of the speaker?_____

    ❑ High-pitched?_____ Normal?_____ Deep pitched?_____

    ❑ Sincere?_____ Rational?_____ Irrational?_____

    ❑ Calm?_____ Angry?_____ Profane?_____

- ❏ Did the call sound LOCAL or LONG DISTANCE?_____
- ❏ Did the callers voice sound FAMILIAR?_____
- ❏ Did the caller ask for a PARTICULAR PERSON?_____
- ❏ As soon as possible, write down what the caller said, **using his or her exact words.**
- ❏ After the call has been completed, you should:*
    - ❏ Call bosses.
    - ❏ Call police.
    - ❏ Call fire department.
    - ❏ Call ambulance service.
    - ❏ Call phone company.
    - ❏ Call electric company.
    - ❏ Call gas company.

Remember that the bomb threat may be real, but the group setting it may not actually want any deaths or injuries. They may be calling to get a lot of publicity for their cause. They may volunteer the name of their group several times, because they want credit for all of these outrages. They may not volunteer the location of the bomb, but if you ask they may tell you, especially if it is a time bomb and you are running out of time. Don't ever be afraid to ask questions in a matter like this. Stay on the phone as long as they do, but get someone in authority to initiate your response plan.

If you receive a bomb threat, search the specific areas at risk very carefully. *Let the professionals do the dangerous work!* Your primary job is to protect people and secondarily your properties. Normally, police, fire, and bomb squad members will have an employee familiar with the facility walk through your buildings. If your institution sponsors a school, for instance, the teacher of a particular classroom could most easily state that "this is not my briefcase, and I don't know who it belongs to. I don't remember it being here before lunch." This would give a focus to the official search.

---

*While all of the after-action list may not be necessary, in some cases it may be. For instance, if there is an explosion, you might have secondary fires or explosions from gas leaks or frayed electric wires. These could be much worse than the primary detonation. Being prepared can make the difference between risk management and catastrophe.

If You Discover a Suspect Package

If you have a package, box, or container that is suspect, don't handle it unnecessarily. The normal approach is to evacuate the premises at this time. Remember, if you can see it, it can see you.[11] It is difficult to know exactly how far away is safe, but as a rule of thumb at least 900 feet in the open (when the device is in line of sight), and 300 feet if you are behind a barricade or have other cover.[12] Monty McGill, a California certified police bomb technician also says to leave the room environment alone.[13] Basically the rundown is this: If the lights in a room are on—leave them on. If the copying machine, computer, and fax are on, leave them on. Don't turn them off. Neither should you turn any equipment on, or turn any lights on, if they were already off. You may set the bomb off, if it was rigged to explode from these devices.

What you *don't do* is as important as what you do. Do not attempt to open the article, nor should you put it in water or in a confined space such as a drawer or cabinet.[14] The water may complete an electronic circuit causing it to detonate. The confined space may increase the amount of shrapnel propelled away, causing more injuries. Perhaps the best thing you can do, other than evacuating, is open the windows in the immediate area to help in venting potential gases.[15]

Endnotes

1. John Douglas and Mark Olshaker, *The Cases that Haunt Us: From Jack the Ripper to JonBenet Ramsey, The FBI's Legendary Mindhunter Sheds Light on the Mysteries That Won't Go Away* (New York: Scribner Publishing, 2000), p. 220.

2. Anti-Defamation League of B'nai Brith, *Security for Community Institutions: A Handbook,* 4th edition, (New York: Anti-Defamation League, 1999), p. 12.

3. Anthony J. Scotti, *Executive Safety and International Terrorism: A Guide for Travelers*, (Englewood Cliffs, N.J.: Prentice Hall Publishers, 1986), p. 97.

4. Paul Fuqua and Jerry V. Wilson, *Terrorism: The Executive's Guide to Survival* (Dallas, Texas: Gulf Publishers, 1978), p. 57.

5. U.S. Department of Commerce, *Survey of Current Business* (Washington, D.C.: U.S. Department of Commerce, August1980), p. 27.

6. Graham Knowles, *Bomb Security Guide* (Los Angeles, Ca.: Security World Publishing Company, 1976), p. 47.

7. Monty McGill [California Certified Police Bomb Technician], "Bombs, Bomb Threats, and Bomb Searches," (Ventura, Ca.: Crisis Consulting International, 1998). This information was originally developed as lesson material for Crisis Consulting International.

8. Graham Knowles, *Bomb Security Guide* (Los Angeles, Ca.: Security World Publishing Company, 1976), p. 57.

9. Graham Knowles, *Bomb Security Guide* (Los Angeles, Ca.: Security World Publishing Company, 1976), p. 47.

10. Anthony J. Sciotti, *Executive Safety and International Terrorism: A Guide for Travelers* (Englewood Cliffs, N.J.: Prentice Hall Publishers, 1986), p. 97.

11. Monty McGill [California Certified Police Bomb Technician], "Bombs, Bomb Threats, and Bomb Searches," (Ventura, Ca.: Crisis Consulting International, 1998). This information was originally developed as lesson material for Crisis Consulting International.

12. Ibid.

13. Ibid.

14. Anti-Defamation League of B'Nai Brith, *Security for Community Institutions: A Handbook*, 4th edition (New York: Anti-Defamation League, 1999), p. 11.

15. Ibid.

CHAPTER 16

COMMITTING TO SECURITY SERVICES

Many of our nation's largest religious facilities have their own proprietary security staff, that is, your institution is the employer. Your institution, church, synagogue, or temple will be responsible for recruiting, selecting, training, and supervising your security staff. Usually proprietary security staffs at religious facilities are after-hours or night watch personnel. Some larger facilities supervise a 24-hour per day security service and include daytime access control responsibilities.

A watch program is fairly easy to administer and usually a facility administrator is given the responsibility for supervising these personnel. However, a comprehensive crime prevention, crime avoidance, and crime deterrence program is a complicated balancing act, not always understood by non-security personnel. Some institutions employ security personnel (proprietary) for around-the-clock services, but use contractual security personnel for worship services and special event management.

If you decide to implement a proprietary program, you will be responsible for all scheduling, including vacations, holidays, and assignments. You will also be responsible for ensuring that your security officers are "state certified" (most, but not all states have security regulatory agencies). You will need to provide bonds, social security, workmens' compensation (matching whatever benefit package your other staff employees have), and a substantial comprehensive insurance program including security protection. You will find that your security personnel are quite costly in terms of liability insurance rates which are based on their (the security officers') gross salaries.

Contractual Security Arrangements

Contractual private security personnel are employees of a separate agency and you pay for their services, usually based on preset hourly fees. *Private security is a profit-oriented industry that provides personnel, equipment, and/or procedures to prevent losses*

Your Institution Should Audit Your Security Contractor's Records On:

- Comprehensive insurance program.
- Certifications on all security officers used at your site.
- All initial training and in-service training programs of the security officers used at your site.
- Workers' compensation policy on all security employees.

caused by human error, emergencies, disasters, or criminal actions[1] Under this arrangement, the private security firm assumes a larger liability than the institution does. Because of liability, your administrators or security committee should review and *audit* the comprehensive security policy of your contractor, the state certificates on each security employee at the time the new employee is employed, certification on all initial training, retraining, and in-service training programs, as well as the workers compensation policy of the contractual firm.

We suggest that it would not be wise to contract with any company with less than a $1,000,000 comprehensive (umbrella) insurance policy. Most well-established security firms have no less than a $5,000,000 policy. Even if your contractual security firm, has such a policy, talk to your facility insurers about insuring the contractual security function as well. While expensive, your institutional policy will greatly reduce your liability if the contractual security agency policy vendor refuses to honor its commitments during a law suit.

> The pros and cons of each type of guard force are the source of endless discussion among security professionals. Proponents of proprietary forces cite the control that the employer has over quality of personnel, better benefits, promotion opportunities, better retention, and so forth. Contract operators counter with arguments about flexibility and economy. Both types of guard forces possess advantages and disadvantages.[2]

Whether your facility uses its own "watch" personnel or not, the security personnel requirements during regular services or special events will be extraordinary. "The choice between proprietary and contract guard services appears to be one of quality control versus flexibility and cost. The decision is not so clear-cut, however. Both proprietary forces and contractor firms *with good management* can meet the needs of your [facility]."[3] While there may be a 24-hour security program manned by one or more personnel simultaneously, the regular services are going to spiral manpower requirements significantly. A church with worship attendance of 5,000 to 7,000 may have 15 to 20 uniformed security officers manning the parking lots, sidewalks, and streets for the several blocks surrounding the facility. If your facility includes plenty of parking spaces, the security personnel are in closer proximity to your members.

A privately funded extension of the public police is the contractual security officer. However, only a fraction of the total private security effort is armed today. Security guards are trained to control access to your properties, continually patrol to detect fires or break-ins, and enforce the rules and regulations established by the institution. In some cases they are authorized to stop, question, and arrest criminal suspects.

It is within this authority, and especially when an authorized weapon is carried, that your liability significantly increases.

Some contractual firms work in security patrol vehicles, traveling from one contract site to another to ensure the security of these premises. Often, the security operation is in concert with burglar and fire alarm operations and central alarm stations owned and operated by the security firm. Some private firms respond immediately upon receiving an alarm of either a break-in or a fire, often arriving even before the police. Others just patrol the businesses who pay their wages, though, by extension, all the businesses in between and around their contracts are more secure because of their intensive patrols, which are in addition to police activity.

If you have parking space limitations, your worship service attendees may park two, three, and even four blocks away. In an inner-city area, these people need to be protected from predators and those who would target their automobiles as they worship. This is when a contract with a good, well-trained, security team can be of great use. Social skills training in the religious institutional environment will be just as important as the security training, insofar as your congregation is concerned.

Advice to Contractual Security Service Providers

Churches, synagogues, mosques, and temples are challenging opportunities for the professional security provider. However, the security consultant or provider may be under some stress when approaching the religious institution. Most are filled with varying customs and practices. Men wear yarmulkes in a synagogue and everyone takes their shoes off in a mosque. All worshipers "cross" themselves upon entering the Roman Catholic church. Priests, nuns, rabbis, and pastors may wear unusual clerical clothes as well. All of this may be confusing for the security provider, especially if he or she comes from a non-religious background. The variances of a Protestant church versus a Catholic church versus a Jewish synagogue may prove bewildering to security providers.

First, let me say not to worry about these variances. If you, as the security provider, are walking into a unique situation, ask the person you are contacting to instruct you on appropriate visitor behavior. Tell him that you have never been in a synagogue, a mosque, or a church of that denomination, and you don't want to violate one of their customs accidentally. They will respect that. They will quickly understand that you don't know much about their group or institution as you interview them for all the information you need to provide a security contract. This would occur anyway. Be up front about it, clear the air, and let them know that you want to respect their customs.

Second, you probably already have the knowledge, skill, and ability (KSA) to provide security for them. You probably have had previous experience in securing stadiums, coliseums, sporting events, concerts, and theatricals. Perhaps you have supplied security for artistic exhibits and for museums. Many of the security skills, both in protecting VIPs, staff, special guests, and paying customers, as well as the assets on premises, are the skills you will need to protect any house of worship. Don't let the clerical clothing and any variance of religious behavior obscure the security tenets that you are already familiar with.

In all likelihood, you will not be able to supply all of their security needs as part of your contract. Recognizing their host of volunteers and being willing to provide security training for these volunteers is appropriate from a business sense, as well as a practical one. You will be more likely to obtain the security contract under these circumstances.

What security do they need the most? Using a divided pyramid as a security paradigm, you can lay the basic groundwork. The security they "must" have will be at the base. This will normally include outside-facility security operations, especially around the parking lots and property perimeters. The next division on your paradigm should be the security they "should" have. Some of these needs can be supplied by a welcoming committee or members dressed in specially marked and colored vests, supplied with cell phones, or at least in-house radio transceivers. The last division of the paradigm should be those security principles which are "nice" to use.

If you are a full-service security service you may choose to offer a segmented bid structure, so that you don't lose out on everything if you don't get the entire contract. Even if you don't get the entire project, but still get some service or sales contracts, you can continue to come back to inspect your goods and services and stay in dialogue with the institution's administration. Perhaps you will get the "entire" contract next time. Occasionally, a small contract leads to increasingly larger responsibilities.

Services Needed Most

- Alarm and alarm supervision.
- CCTV installation and supervision.
- Contractual security patrol services.
- Uniformed security services before, during, and after worship services.
- Personnel investigations of staff members and volunteers working in sensitive positions and especially with children.

The way religious institutions make purchasing and contractual decisions is unique. No one church, synagogue, or mosque will be the same. Even within "like faiths," there may be considerable difference. When you try to market your contract, try to find out who you will be dealing with, and if that person will make the final decision, of if a committee, or the congregation will make it. Some purchasing and contractual decisions can be authorized beforehand by the membership, others must be approved after all the bids are in.

This isn't much different than working with many large businesses and corporations. Get the name and telephone number of the person you should contact and call them back after an appropriate period. If you didn't get the contract, find out why. You may be able to improve your bid in the next contract period. Worship center security offers a valued service in our society.

Endnotes

1. Karen M. Hess and Henry M. Wrobleski, *Introduction to Private Security* 2nd ed., (Saint Paul, Minn.: West Publishing Company, 1988), p. 25.

2. Lucien G. Canton, Guard Force Management, (Boston, Butterworth-Heinemann Publishers, 1996), p. 5.

3. Ibid.

Part IV:
General Crime Prevention

CHAPTER 17

SEXUAL HARASSMENT

This problem can occur anywhere at your facility. From the administrative offices, to the teaching complex, the music program or to the janitorial staff. One church in the mid-South learned the hard way.[1] The church had a congregation of about 1,200 and a full staff of associate pastors, music ministry personnel, organists, pianists, and three janitors. One of the janitors was a female.

She had been fully employed by the church for several years, working closely with her male associates. During a period of instability, when the pastor had resigned and several associate pastors sought positions in other churches, she told the sexual harassment officer of her state's Equal Employment Opportunity Commission (EEOC) that one of the other janitors had made inappropriate sexual remarks to her. She also claimed that he had nude calendars in the janitorial services' locker room, which embarrassed her.

She told EEOC that she had reported these problems to a church staff member who was now serving in another church and living in another state, as well as telling the church (lay) trustee who had supervisory authority over the janitorial staff. This claim was disputed by all of the trustees and the former associate pastor. They denied that she had reported any of these issues prior to the EEOC complaint.

However, the church staff was not given more credibility because of their role or position. The word of one woman, against the word of senior ordained staff and lay leaders in the church was accepted. The church representatives were treated in a cavalier and patronizing manner, even to the point of being interrupted by the hearing officer when they were trying to dispute her claims. The EEOC ruled against the church, and in the female janitor's behalf. The case then went from a confidential government administrative hearing into the civil court system. The janitor was going to sue. To keep the matter from "going public" and being disruptive within their fellowship, the church settled this dispute outside of court for an undisclosed figure.

Definition

Sexual harassment—we all know what it is, but few can define it. Generally, sexual harassment is defined as an unwelcome sexual advance, a request for sexual favors, or other verbal or physical conduct of a sexual nature. Sexual harassment is always inappropriate. In the United States it is unlawful, having no place in secular institutions, much less religious ones.

Religious leaders need to recognize the structure of EEOC. The agency is multi-tiered, including local, state, and Federal agencies. Often, after a sustained finding on the local level, the victim will file a litigation suit in court, seeking compensatory damages. This brings a tremendous amount of embarrassment to the local congregation. It harms credibility and causes people to question the community of believers. EEOC has broad jurisdiction and may choose to publish their findings as a method of bringing attention to their services and function. The EEOC has broad investigative powers, as well as a judicial function.

A Law Violation Occurs When:

- Submission to such conduct is made explicit or implicitly a condition of employment.
- Submission to or rejection of such conduct is used as a basis for an employment decision affecting such individual.
- If such conduct has the purpose or effect of unreasonably interfering with an individual's work performance or creating an intimidating, hostile, or offensive working environment.

While gathering material to write this book, we learned of many situations involving unethical sexual practices in the church. A pastor was charged with rape at church. A married church secretary ran away with her pastor. Homes and lives were destroyed. The church membership felt betrayed.

It is difficult to discern sexual harassment. However, we can deal with it vigorously. The church needs a published harassment policy, both for the membership and the staff. When a new staff member is employed, he or she should read and sign the policy and this statement should be maintained in the personnel file. The policy should be posted in areas where employees can see it. This will reduce the church's liability and will offer the staff member the opportunity to solve the issue "inside the fellowship" before going outside or to the EEOC.

We wish there was a way to screen sexual harassers or potential harassers. The psychologist who develops this personality profile evaluation will be rewarded. Remember that anyone can be a harasser: male or female, young or old, attractive or unattractive. Having a policy statement and a way to address the problem will go a long way in helping you defend a harassment claim.

Increasingly, the harassment issue is becoming prevalent in houses of worship. As the role of the religious institution expands, there is increasing opportunity for these crimes. Many churches run service businesses for their congregations and when job openings exist in day care or schools, they allow nonmember families to participate. Churches that run preschools, schools, daytime activity programs, after-school study programs, and those that have extensive active programs must employ personnel from within and from without the organization to staff these positions. This increases the possibility that these charges can be filed—whether true—or false.

See the table for suggestions on how staff and volunteers can avoid even the appearance of inappropriate behavior. It is difficult to associate harassment with worship and worshipers, but, on occasion, this activity occurs in worship centers. Sometimes the behavior is subtle and sometimes it is blatant. While we prefer to think that a pastor, priest, rabbi, or minister would not be a participant, we must realize that it does happen on occasion. Our goal is to be proactive—to recognize it and to respond appropriately.

Suggestions on How to Avoid the Appearance of Inappropriate Behavior When Counseling, Visiting, or Meeting with Members of the Opposite Sex

- Start each visit with prayer and/or meditation.
- Be sure someone else is in an office, close by.
- Keep your physical distance and avoid touching.
- Keep the doors open.
- Do not have an extended meeting or session.
- If additional counseling is needed, schedule an appointment in your office when your secretary is present.
- If counseling, take detailed notes including arrival and departure time.

Endnotes

1. From an anonymous source. Because of potential injury to the ministry and secondary victimization issues, we choose not to identify this church.

CHAPTER 18

CRIME PREVENTION AT A MEGA-FACILITY

The co-authors of this book have visited numerous churches, synagogues, and mosques across the country. The research for this book has been compiled over many years and encompasses many religions, denominations, and criminal acts. We have observed numerous programs and procedures that have been put into practice because of past criminal attacks or the fear of future criminal activity. Based on our experiences and the interviews at these facilities, we believe we can speak with authority about the positives and negatives of these programs.

In 2000, we both had the privilege to tour and attend Southeast Christian Church, one of the largest churches in the United States, large in both membership and physical size. While we were in awe of the beauty and the size of the complex, we were also impressed with the crime prevention strategies they had implemented and with the security professional who directed the crime prevention and asset protection programs.

Southeast is peacefully located on 100 acres of land, just off of a busy expressway in Louisville, Kentucky. The parking lot is accessible by five entrances and the church is surrounded by 4,625 parking spaces. The church averages over 15,000 attendees each weekend for the Saturday evening service and two Sunday morning services. During the annual Easter Pageant, over 76,000 people attend during a two-week period, so there are periods of intensive attendance, as well as large crowds on Saturdays and Sundays.

The sanctuary was designed to ensure a feeling of closeness for the 9,000 seats on the tiered levels of five floors. The parking lots were designed around the building to reduce the walk. The atrium was designed to be open and vast to encourage communication. The classrooms were designed to allow observation from the hallway as each door has a window and a long narrow side window from top to bottom.

Child care rooms have open views and security cameras are strategically placed. The offices of the ministers were placed in an area that has limited access through a hallway choke point with a strategically placed camera system. The vault was placed in an inconspicuous area and it has several layers of protection, both technological and by personnel.

You may wonder why a church would take such precautions? We asked the same question and discovered that the church had encountered only minor incidents in the past. For example, they had several occasions where the security staff would find individuals sleeping in the parking lot during the night. On one occasion, someone came in and stole several purses from the offices. This does not appear to be a major high-crime area. However, it is important to remember that the potential for victimization is great unless we take precautions and are proactive in our approach.

This facility is open seven days a week from early morning to late evening. The complex includes a bookstore, gym, food pantry, and separate business offices for the music ministry, newspaper staff, and the pastoral unit. Scheduling is complicated here, with many events and classes offered during the week in various parts of the buildings. We mention this to highlight the vulnerability. The mere size of the building and the services offered increase the potential for victimization. Knowing this, the designers and church leaders took extra precautions and we applaud them for their efforts.

In addition to the carefully designed buildings and campus, the administrators formed a group of security personnel called "Nehemiah's Team." This name was selected based on the biblical account of the Prophet Nehemiah who was given the opportunity to rebuild the temple of Jerusalem. Enemies threatened the construction site. Sanballat, Tobiah, the Arabians, the Ammonites, and the Ashdodites wanted to stop the rebuilding. The scripture says, "They were very wroth."[1] After learning of their conspiracy through intelligence gathering,[2] the Israelites "prayed" and then "set up a watch."[3] The watch was carefully coordinated. Nehemiah assigned men to the lower walls of Jerusalem and to the upper walls.[4] Nehemiah said that, he "even set the people after their families, with their swords, their spears, and their bows."[5] As the work proceeded, half the men guarded the wall,[6] and the men who built the wall "had his sword girded by his side."[7]

The minister of Southeast Christian Church asked for volunteers who had special skills and experience in handling adversity. They quickly discovered that they had over 30 peace officers in their membership who were willing to give their time and resources to church protection and crime prevention. Peace officers in their state are authorized to carry guns and to make arrests at any location. Each member of "Nehemiah's Team" has an assigned seat during services (some are even in the choir loft) and they are strategically placed in the congregation to provide protection in the event a guest becomes disruptive or has less than desirable intentions.

In addition to the "Nehemiah's Team" placement during the services, the church has hired over 30 local uniformed peace officers who are given assignments outside to direct traffic, patrol the parking lots in their patrol vehicles, and to respond where appropriate during services. This is a tremendous benefit to the church because it helps to ensure that the cars are not vandalized and that traffic will move quickly as members abide by the traffic director's rules. The church considers security personnel as an outreach ministry because many of the officers will attend service while waiting to direct traffic after the service. Many have decided to join the church and now consider it home. Others have encouraged their family and friends to attend also.

In addition to "Nehemiah's Team," many of the law enforcement officers volunteer as "Door Keepers" who serve as part of the welcoming committee. They are dressed in civilian clothing and do not depict a "police" presence. However, in the event of an emergency, they are armed and ready to respond.

While developing security procedures, they decided to include a section for emergency medical services. A congregation of this size will most certainly have problems during each service. People may faint, fall down the stairs, give birth to babies, experience heart attacks and strokes, or a host of other problems. When designing the facility, they designated five first-aid rooms located throughout the facility, but the primary triage unit is easily accessible from the sanctuary. These rooms include medical supplies, phones, alarms, and more to ensure the safety of those attending the services.

Again, the minister appealed for volunteers and discovered that the congregation had many members of the health care profession including nurses, doctors, physician aides, and emergency technicians. At the time of this writing, they reported responding to at least one "call" per service, covering events like sprained ankles, allergic reactions, and heart attacks. The church pays for an on-site ambulance to stand by during each service in case of the need for emergency transport. Unfortunately, during one evening service, a woman suffered a heart attack and died.

Tithes and Offerings

A church of this size has a tremendous offering with a great deal of cash coming in at least two times a week. There are very strict policies about how the money is collected, stored, sorted, counted, and deposited. When the offering is transported from the sanctuary to the vault, there is a security cadre accompanying it to decrease the risk of theft. When the money is counted for deposit purposes, there are a specific number of people involved. Additionally, deposits are made with the assistance of a security firm.

One particularly observant feature the church staff has implemented is a newly designed offering plate. The offering plate has a metal frame that is connected to a heavy, multi-layered cloth bag. This accomplishes two things. First, it does not reveal to a thief how much money is in the offering bag without peering down into the bag, which would be obvious. Secondly, a thief would have to reach down in the bag to palm some money. The traditional offering plate offers a quick opportunity to "lift" money, particularly if an accomplice creates a disturbance as the plate is passed because all eyes turn to the disturbance, while the theft is in progress.

Radio Communications/CCTV Office

The church owns over 60 walkie-talkie radios and issues them at each service to the officers directing traffic, members of the *Nehemiah Team*, the medical team, and other staff. The radios have a cross-band operator that allows immediate notification on all radios regardless of channel. This is important because the specialty unit has a restricted channel. If medical is needed in the nursery, they are just a radio call away. If someone needs to be escorted out of the building, it is just a radio call away.

Security for the Minister

The architects of Southeast Christian Church designated several routes by which the minister can exit his office to arrive in the sanctuary. Additionally, they included an area where he could stay should a disruption occur. The room is equipped with emergency equipment and phones. The building includes routes by which the minister leaves the pulpit and arrives at the other end of the building without moving through the crowd. This accomplishes several things. It allows him to move effortlessly throughout the building and allows him to be on time for the next scheduled event. If he were to walk from one area to the other among the congregation, he would be surrounded by people and would be expected to shake hands for hours or someone would complain that he isn't friendly. A security officer who watches the crowd accompanies the minister as he moves from area to area. The security officer is constantly watching to protect him should someone attempt to harm him physically or to create a scene. This is accomplished in a very professional manner and to the average person it is completely unobtrusive.

Conclusion

We know that every facility cannot afford all of the security approaches employed at the Southeast Christian Church. However, every facility and religious institution can develop security policies, security procedures, and a "church watch." Chapter 3 on security and crime prevention planning offers various suggestions, some of which do not cost a great deal, but can have a strong impact in your crime prevention and crime reduction efforts.

Endnotes

1. Neh. 4:7, Authored (King James) Version.

2. Neh. 4:8, (AV).

3. Neh. 4:9, (AV).

4. Neh. 4:13, (AV).

5. Neh. 4:13, (AV).

6. Neh. 4:16, (AV).

7. Neh. 4:18, (AV).

CHAPTER 19

WHAT CHURCHES CAN DO ABOUT CRIME AT CHURCH AND IN THE COMMUNITY

Throughout history, the church has served various roles including both a sanctuary and an asylum. In the Middle Ages, churches and monasteries were exempt from taxes and laws that affected others, and were granted an immunity. During the Reformation, measures were passed to restrict these privileges and to end their abuses because the asylum given by churches and monasteries posed a threat to the normal administration of justice. People who had committed crimes would often seek refuge in church buildings because of the sanctuary provisions.

History provides numerous accounts of individuals seeking refuge. However, there are few, if any accounts, of any criminal activity that these individuals committed while residing under the protection of the church. Do we reach the conclusion that each person was miraculously converted from his or her life of crime? Based on the research associated with this book, we would conclude that the church exercised extreme caution not to release this information in fear that it would reflect poorly on the spirituality of the leaders and those who lived in the facility.

If someone within our midst commits a violent act, do we blame the church? Has the church failed to provide proper guidance? Does it mean that we are less spiritual than the church down the street? Is it a reflection on our teaching? As religious administrators, we must examine these questions and equalize the impact of crime. We must accept the fact that if individuals associated with a church resort to crime, it is not a reflection on your ministry. However, the methods in which you respond are reflective on your ministry.

If we base our actions on avoidance, then we have failed to provide comfort and healing to the victims and the family members who are often devastated. If we seek forgiveness for the action and work to avoid the legal system, then we have failed to adhere to the justice system and establish a pattern of activity. We must place responsibility on the persons who commit the crime and hold them accountable to the community, the religious teachings, and the law of the land.

In many instances, church leaders are faced with situations that they do not want to report to the authorities because they fear retaliation or that people will stop attending, or that others will come forward with similar allegations. However, this is not unique to churches. This is also true of crimes that occur on college campuses, in shopping malls, hospitals, etc.

One hindrance to reporting crime is the fear of retaliation. We fear that if the charges are dismissed, the person or a family member will retaliate. We fear civil suits. If a church employee is accused of a crime or of inappropriate conduct, we fear that society will believe that the church is being discriminatory in its practices and is not effective in its preemployment screening. We do not want people to believe that individuals receive a lesser punishment because the church supported them or asked for special consideration. We fear the effectiveness of our teachings will be challenged.

If church crimes are reported, we may believe that people will stop attending out of fear of being the next victim. We fear that if we admit that people have been victimized, people will not want to visit our establishments. The fear of crime is very real for many of us in our daily lives. We lock our doors. We carry canisters of mace. We take extra precautions to reduce the potential of victimization. We feel vulnerable and we remember incidents that have occurred in particular areas. If we know of an area that is a "hot spot" we avoid it like the plague. We'll change our routine and vary our schedules in an effort to feel more secure. If our feeling of safety has been violated while at church, then we may opt to avoid the setting.

In a church setting, if people do not feel safe, they may stop attending services or may participate on a very limited basis. If the elderly do not feel safe at night, then they may stop attending night services. If people do not feel safe to pray in the building during the day, then they may discontinue this activity. If they stop attending church, then chances are they will limit their donations or stop donating their financial resources. If this happens, the church will suffer financially and could be forced to close the doors. If people stop participating in the activities, it could influence others to quit and, therefore, would hinder the growth and effectiveness of the church.

Second, if people do not feel safe, they may question the sincerity of the church leaders and may "misplace the blame" on others. They may blame the leader for the crimes that are occurring because they believe that the leaders should know what is going on and they should be keeping a "better eye" on their members. They may decide that the crime is a reflection on the lifestyle of the leaders.

Third, they may question the spirituality and the teachings of the church. "If the church ministers and leaders were living according to the scriptures and teachings, then these things would not happen," say some victims. Some people often associate the crime with the victim and assume that it was the victim's fault. Blame is often placed on the victim and it is viewed as a "lesson." They may conclude that if the church leaders were doing the right thing then bad things would not happen.

Additionally, administrators may be hesitant to talk about some types of crime for fear there are other victims that they do not know about. Others may not have come forward or reported their victimization. Additionally, we believe that it reflects poorly on our decision-making abilities and indicates that we are not doing an adequate job in the screening process. For example, if we have a Bible class teacher who has been accused of sexually assaulting a student, there is no way to know if there have been other victims. However, if this person is exposed, then there may be other victims who would be willing to come forward with their story.

A pastor was arrested in Kentucky, charged with rape of a woman who visited his office. In Texas, a married missionary lady told one co-author about being raped in her van after a "nice" deacon offered to help her carry mission and country-specific materials to her vehicle. In this case, the church was split. The deacon denied the criminal charges. Some members believed the deacon, others believed the missionary lady as they discussed the accusations in open business meetings. Some members left the church in silent protest over this event.

Often, it is difficult for one person to come forward because of the fears that his or her story will not be believed or that people will blame the victim for the crime. This is especially evident when key church leaders are charged with crimes against members or guests. Society often blames the victim and victims are often hesitant to come forward. Depending on the number of individuals who come forward, the church may suffer from a decline in attendance or offerings. The leaders may be ridiculed and asked to resign.

Generally, crimes such as monetary theft and embezzling are not reported to law enforcement agencies and are usually only shared with the board members. Why is this? We believe there is a general tendency to protect the congregation. If you believe the money was stolen by an "insider" then you are less likely to have the perpetrator arrested. It reflects poorly on the checks and balances that the financial department has put into place. There are several reasons that churches do not prosecute insiders including a belief that the person will return the money, and a belief that the person will correct the wrong deed and do the "right" thing. Additionally, the "insider" criminal may be protected because church leaders do not want the congregation thinking that they are lax in the safekeeping of the tithe and offerings.

Another area that is likely to be unreported is an incident involving drugs or alcohol. If the church teaches against the use of these substances, then it is more likely to be ignored and "swept under the carpet." This is because if we focus on the subject, then we are exposing the usage and that may reflect poorly on those who attend the services. We are failing in our mission if we have not changed behaviors and lifestyles.

Crimes such as arson and burglary are more likely to be committed by a stranger and it doesn't reflect as poorly as a crime committed by a member. If our facility is burglarized, then we are likely to report it to the law enforcement authorities because the insurance will likely replace whatever was stolen, plus burglary is usually committed by someone "outside." This crime, unlike crimes such as sexual assaults, date rape, and child molestation, is more likely to be reported because of the fear that it instills in everyone's mind. However, the fear of being a victim could have a detrimental effect on the stability and growth of the church.

As an administrator, it is imperative that as soon as something is reported, you take immediate action, investigate the claim to the fullest extent and, if necessary, consult your local law enforcement agency. You must be willing to accept the fact that regardless of the outcome someone will lose. Whether it is the victim or the perpetrator, reputations will be destroyed and you will spend many hours dealing with the allegations, investigation, and the results

It is sometimes difficult to cast aside our "blinders" and look at crime from the criminological perspective. Whether we are dealing with teenage drinking, sexual perversions, or embezzling, we are often surrounded by individuals who are prone to commit crime. The criminological theories offer various explanations. Religion offers others. Whether we believe that men are innately evil or whether we believe that men are born good and society causes them to commit crime, the explanations and theories can be debated at great length. Regardless of your belief on the causes of crime, we must conclude that there is a role for the church in the area of crime prevention.

The Church's Role When a Member Commits a Crime

Often we ask the question, how did we let the "member predator" slip through our fingers? It is not a matter of slipping through the fingers; it is often a matter of letting go of the hand. First, we must accept the act and focus on the behavior. The person must be willing to accept responsibility for his actions and must be willing to make restitution if feasible. On the other hand, the church must be willing to hold him accountable and not brush the incident under the carpet. Administrators must accept and acknowledge the behavior and focus on ways to correct the behavior.

Second, we must seek ways to correct the behavior. The individual must realize that he has committed a crime and must know that what he did was wrong and must take steps to keep it from happening again. Additionally, we must provide alternatives. Helping the individual to focus energies on other projects will help to eliminate the opportunity to commit additional crimes.

Third, in some instances we must not chastise the perpetrator, but we must reach out in love and support. Chastising the perpetrator will only perpetuate more hatred and disapproval, which could result in lower self-esteem and a repetition of the deviant behavior.

A common solution utilized by agencies throughout the country is the concept of keeping individuals busy. If your community is experiencing teenage crime, then it is imperative that the local worship centers become involved in ways to keep teenagers focused on other activities. This is why youth activity leagues and prom night parties are very popular and successful.

When a Nonmember Commits a Church Crime: Responses?

Should the church reach out to people who have victimized the church? Should the church become involved in hearings and court proceedings? If someone becomes active in religious teachings, does that mean that we are to forgive his behavior and excuse him from responsibility? If each perpetrator seeks repentance, is that enough? Is it necessary to involve law enforcement? We will not attempt to address these issues; however, we encourage individuals to work in partnership with their local law enforcement agencies and court systems.

It is amazing the number of individuals who are in prison and suddenly "find" religion. This is usually the first thing they want to discuss with the parole board. While we are not questioning the sincerity of their experiences, still it appears rather convenient that discussing the experience could have an impact on the amount of time spent inside the prison. Additionally, individuals arrested for driving while impaired often find religion and seek leniency from the courts.

As an administrator, how will you respond when someone commits a crime against someone in your fellowship and later accepts the teachings of the congregation? Does his acceptance of the faith excuse previous behavior? Should he be punished in a court of law? Should he be held accountable? These are theological questions that individuals have debated for years and we will not attempt to provide a summary. However, it is noted that these questions can split a congregation because of differences of opinion and varying interpretations of the scriptures.

How Can Congregations Influence Crime Prevention?

In our efforts to evangelize and experience growth in our congregations, have we looked closely at our community and the problems that are surrounding our four walls? Is the building located in an area that is plagued with drugs and alcohol? Do the police make frequent visits in the neighborhood responding to domestic violence or shootings? What are the issues surrounding the building and how can we be involved?

We strongly recommend that your congregation work with your local law enforcement agency. Your enforcement officers can do several things for you. First, they can provide a security assessment of your facility. Secondly, they can tell you about crime in your area. Third, their presence and interest can often serve as a deterrent to criminal activity. Fourth, they can work with you to develop security programs for the protection of your church.

After the major crime risks have been identified, you can then develop an action plan to address those crimes. The action plan can be developed in conjunction with your religious beliefs and can be applicable to your outreach programs. There is a nondenominational group in Louisville, Kentucky, that holds prayer vigils every weekend in part of the city's west end in an attempt to stop the drug dealing and shootings. This small group of eight to 10 people walk the streets and stand on the street corners while having prayer. They approach people who are dealing drugs and invite them to participate in their worship services. This outreach has been ongoing for the last several years. The group is confident that they have made a positive impact and that you can see the difference in the community.

A Protestant minister relayed this story to his congregation one Sunday morning. He told about an old maid that lived alone and was becoming feeble. Every night she prayed for her neighborhood and prayed that the liquor store on the corner, which was a haven for drug dealers and drunks, would burn down. For years, she repeated this prayer every night. As she continued to grow older, she decided to have someone move in with her. The first night during devotions, she repeated her prayer to her new roommate and told how desperately she wanted her prayer to be answered.

The next morning, to her disbelief, she found that the liquor store had burned to the ground. She asked her roommate about her faith and remarked how strong she must be to have prayed only one night and the building burned to the ground. Her new roommate remarked with a brief smile, "Sometimes, you've got to put legs on your prayers." We are not advocating "putting legs on your prayers." We do advocate that people become more aware of their community and look for ways to solve problems collectively.

One Baptist congregation in Louisville, Kentucky, identified the availability of alcohol as one of the biggest problems in their community. "Mom and Pop" liquor stores, located on nearly every corner, made it easy for individuals to stop off and spend their paycheck before going home. They also noticed that people were loitering in the street around the liquor stores. They also knew the damage that alcohol was doing to many of the local families. So, the congregation decided to rid the community of the liquor stores. They went, one-by-one, and purchased the liquor stores. They either tore the building down or rehabilitated it into some other type of service such as child care facilities, barber shops, etc.

Working Together: Congregations, Pastors, Priests, Rabbis, and Police Officers

Many communities across the nation are placing emphasis on a policing style called "community oriented policing." This style of policing places greater emphasis on community relations and encourages law enforcement officers to be more involved in the communities they are serving and to be more accessible. It encourages partnerships between the community and the police department and improves the lines of communication. It also improves the probability that law enforcement can solve crimes because members of the community are willing to talk. This creates a win-win situation for law enforcement and the community. Not only are crimes being solved, they can be solved much faster due to the cooperation of the community leaders.

A nondenominational group in Louisville decided to work with the police department in identifying drug dealers and gang members. They made several visits to the local jail to talk with gang members trying to learn more about the leaders and the illegal activities. It has yet to be determined if this program will be successful.

There are many ways in which the police agencies can coordinate activities with your congregation. For example, they can fingerprint children. They can teach seniors about crimes against the elderly. They can teach college students and women about personal safety. They can assist the church in completing a safety check. All of these are vital services offered by your local police department. You are encouraged to reach out and form crime prevention partnerships to solve the crime problems in your area.

CHAPTER 20

CONCLUSION

Reading this book is the first step in preventing crime in your place of worship. As you have read the many accounts, we know that you have been shocked at the reality of what has occurred and we hope that you are concerned with the possibility of what could occur at your facility. That is why we wrote this book.

Crime prevention cannot be measured because there is no way to predict what could happen. However, we do know that there are ways to prevent crime. As we have worked in both the law enforcement field, as well as the security profession, we have talked often with criminals about what makes an easy target. We have covered those areas thoroughly in this book. Locks, lights, visibility, neighborhood watches, alarms, etc. create an unfriendly environment to the criminal, thereby removing your facility from the "Easy Target" list.

However, writing the book and your subsequent reading of this book is simply the first step. It is imperative that you take action and implement some, if not all, of the recommendations in this book. Each congregation will review crime in a different way and each congregation, based on size, location, financial resources, and beliefs will respond in a different way. We do not know the vulnerable areas in your facility and that is why we referred you to your local law enforcement agency for assistance. We also encouraged you to work with your insurance company and its risk deterrence personnel. If your insurer will provide a percentage discount for security measures, it may not take too many years to pay for the initial investment.

We acknowledge that implementing the recommendations in this book can seem overwhelming. That's why we encourage you to accomplish these changes in phases. If you identify and correct the most vulnerable areas first, then you can focus on other issues later as additional resources become available.

Overcoming the paradigms of your membership may be one of the most difficult tasks. It is often difficult for members to understand the need for change. This book will assist you in those efforts as we have highlighted many incidents of crime. As we explored the precautions used by businesses, schools, shopping centers and our homes, we stressed the vulnerability of our worship facilities and provided valid examples of victimizations.

Granted, there are many ways to accomplish the recommendations. It may be necessary to reach a compromise in some situations and we encourage that "some protection is better than no protection." If your congregation will not agree to lock the sanctuary doors during the day, perhaps you can convince them of the need to lock the doors at night and on holidays when facilities are extremely vulnerable. As your members accept these security programs incrementally, it will be easier to become more restrictive as time passes.

If your congregation will agree to purchase a safe, then it will be easier to agree on locking procedures. If your membership will change the hiring procedures, then it will be easier to screen applicants with criminal record checks. Accepting a major security program may be a difficult and unfulfilling task because we cannot see results immediately. Over time, however, these approaches will be both cost effective and people-friendly.

We encourage open communication with your members and encourage you to share information with them as you learn more about crime in places of worship. Newspapers across the country continue to report crimes in places of worship. It is not a new phenomenon. As we were completing this work, new crimes occurred which we could not incorporate. For example, a man was convicted of a church bombing in Alabama that killed four people, and two women were shot and killed during a church service in Kentucky. The examples you find may be small in number, but when viewed as a whole, crime continues leaving congregations hurt by the experience.

If your congregation is a member of a larger organization in other states or countries, we encourage you to establish a task force in which you collect information annually and present it to the membership or to a committee. The sharing of information is the growth of knowledge.

We must work diligently to protect our sacred places. We have experienced various traditions in our facilities and they contain sacred artifacts. These are places where our parents married, our babies were christened, and our lives influences. The statutes, Bibles, Torahs, and Korans can never be replaced if destroyed or stolen. We owe it to our members and to future generations to preserve our worship heritage and to protect our places of worship.

ABOUT THE AUTHORS

Chester L. Quarles, CPP, has worked extensively within the security industry since 1973, both in his security firm in north Mississippi and with Crisis Consulting International, a volunteer group of security professionals serving the international missionary community. He has served as a U.S. Army military policeman and as the director of the Mississippi Bureau of Narcotics. Dr. Quarles is a professor in the Criminal Justice Program of the University of Mississippi. He received his Ph.D. in Criminal Justice Administration from Sam Houston State University. He is the author of several books.

Paula L. Ratliff earned her B.S. and M.S. in Justice Administration from the University of Louisville. She began researching crimes against religious facilities in the early 1990s and completed her Master's thesis on the victimization of religious facilities in 1995. That same year, she was chosen as the Outstanding Graduate Student of the Year by the Southern Criminal Justice Association and presented a paper on victimization of religious facilities at the association's annual conference. She has written several articles on crime prevention for places of worship and other topics. She is employed as the human resources administrator/director for the Jefferson County Corrections Department in Jefferson County, Kentucky.